Create a
FUNCTIONAL
RESUME

'How to' Learner Guide and
Activity Workbook for newbie
and struggling job-seekers

the *Savvy Jobseeker Academy* and
CHAR MESAN

Create a FUNCTIONAL RESUME

First published in 2015
© 2015 Char Mesan

Char Mesan Enterprises
Penrith NSW 2750
Australia
ABN 51 0887 646 671

http://charmessanjobtraining.blogspot.com.au
http://thesavvyjs.blogspot.com.au

National Library of Australia
Catagoguing-in-Publication entry:
Mesan, Char
Create a Functional Resume

ISBN 13: 978-0-9942137-2-3

Notice of Liability

Book Interior:	Char Mesan
Cover Design:	Char Mesan Charmaine Quinlivan
Transcription:	S.P Trevor
Images:	pixaby.com, tooncharacters.com

10 9 8 7 6 5 4 3 2 1

Table of CONTENTS

Firstly, WELCOME!

Hello, my name is Char Mesan.

I teach frustrated and struggling jobseekers how to fix up their failing resumes, cover letters, statements addressing selection criteria and improve their general jobseeking practices so they start gaining success at progressing past hiring managers initial readthroughs, and snag those job interviews and ultimately nail the job they want to gain.

And, I teach those new to jobseeking how they can avoid making all the unnecessary mistakes and pitfalls that when present just sets them on that long one-way trip towards Rejectionville and where they end up taking residence on Struggle Street or Frustration Alley.

I'm your Instructor throughout this entire course. And I don't want you wasting time or doing it financially tough for a moment longer than is absolutely necessary.

Here's how I'm going to help you.

In this course, I will teach you how to use effective written communication skills and solid resume writing techniques so that your job applications will capture the hiring managers' attention, pass their initial readthrough review and progress to the next stage in their hiring process because you've caused the decision maker to view you as potentially suitable for the role and a good fit to their vacancy.

I'm going to teach you how to do all this in the most comprehensive, easy to understand and follow method on the planet, so you gain fast, successful results towards gaining the job you want.

And maybe even have a bit of fun along the way.

About this BOOK

This **'How to' Learner Guide and Activity Workbook** print publication is an amalgamation of the PDF Student (Activity) Workbook, the video transcripts of each of the lessons and tutorials, and a small selection from the many graphics used to create the video-tutorials, from the training course, **'How to Create a Functional Resume'**, created for and offered by the $\mathcal{S}$avvy $\mathcal{J}$obseeker $\mathcal{A}$cademy.

So, while this publication uses Australian English spelling, and conforms to the rules for punctuation (except where mistakes and typographical errors make their way into this work), there will be many incidents where sentences are not grammatically correct, and slang and jargon is used.

Also, we designed this print publication with the view that you can write in it, so we have inserted the relevant workbook activities into the correlating lessons, to make it easy for you to complete the activities along the way.

Course OVERVIEW

You have chosen the functional resume format as the best fit for your job type and personal background, and like many jobseekers, you probably have some application weaknesses to overcome.

That's okay, because I'll show you what to do and how to go about writing your resume; In the lessons section, I'll guide you on how to decide on the sections and the specifics to include, and, most importantly, I'll share resume writing tips and hiring insights that will enable you to leverage your strengths, lower the impact of your employability weaknesses and set yourself apart from the majority in a positive, compelling way.

I have worked with jobseekers for over 10 years and have consistently had them tell me that the problems they experience when it comes to writing a resume, for them, boils down to not knowing these things.

Not knowing:

- what to write
- where to start
- how to go about it
- what sections and specifics to include
- what sections and specifics not to include
- how to set themself apart from other applicants
- how to show their value / benefits / strengths
- how to market themselves effectively
- how to make their application more interesting and appealing to employers
- how to lessen the impact their weaknesses has on their employability
- if they are providing too much or too little detail

Do you identify with any of those?

I think you'll agree: that's a whole lot of not knowing for an activity that is so important and directly impacts upon the state of our health and wealth-iness.

And that not-knowing stops for you right now.

By the end of this course, you will be able to:

- Understand how the Hiring Manager reviews your application
- Learn which resume sections to build content for
- Decide whether a specific detail is relevant to be included in the section you are working on or to leave it out
- Ensure each detail is then optimised for maximum Hiring Manager interest and best demonstrates your value, benefits and strengths

- Know how to target your resume – and any future updates to it – so that the applications you submit will appeal to the widest range of potential employers as you can make it

To learn all this, you'll find this course has 3 core modules, each with multiple lessons and tutorials.

These are:

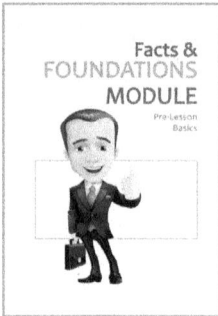

- Facts & Foundations: Pre-lesson Basics
- Formulate: Develop your Content
- Finalise with Finesse: Post-lesson Finishing Touches

Facts & Foundations: Pre-lesson Functional Resume Basics – Before you begin creating the content for your resume, you first need to understand the basics of the Functional Format so that you work to this format's strengths and can minimise its weaknesses. This section briefly discusses the most important aspects.

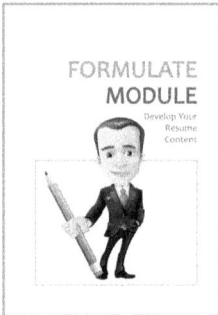

Formulate: Develop your resume Content – This is where the fun and interactive part begins. In this section, you will get to the heart of creating the content of a quality resume that even the toughest hiring managers are happy to read and will cause them to believe in your suitability to their vacancy needs.

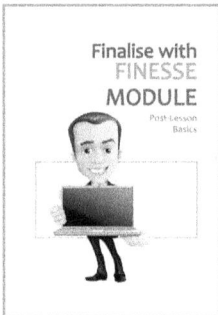

Finalise with Finesse: Post-lesson Finishing Touches – This is where we tie up loose ends to finalise your resume with finesse. Everything you'll have learned this far has been about getting you to demonstrate quality, effective written communication skills and resume writing techniques. Now, you just need to finish off with the little things that can make all the difference.

We will use the video tutorials in conjunction with the Student Workbook, which you will find in the Facts & Foundations section.

You will find a dedicated space for each lesson in the Student Workbook where you can take notes. I'll ask that you complete activities as you progress – not leave them for later – and that you do them in the order given.

Not sure if the FUNCTIONAL RESUME FORMAT is right for you?

Before students enrol in a the *Savvy Jobseeker Academy* resume course, we ask students to complete our short training course, **'What TYPE of Resume Do You Need?'** to make sure our job seeking clients don't start their looking for work off on the wrong foot by using a resume that is not suitable to their particular personal background and job role.

As a purchasers of the transcripts of our **How to Create a Functional Resume** course, if you would like to ensure that creating a Functional Format resume is indeed the right one for you, you are welcome to head on over to our blog website or Facebook Page and follow the links to that course before you proceed further, if you like, so that you too get that part right.

You'll find links to the free course, and others, at:

> **the *Savvy Jobseeker Academy***
> http://thesavvyjs.blogspot.com.au
>
> **Char Mesan Resumes & Jobsearch Training**
> http://charmesanjobtraining.blogspot.com.au
>
> **Facebook Page**
> The Savvy Jobseeker Academy
> Char Mesan

Your ONE THING

Before you begin the lessons, I want you to take a few moments right now and think about why you are here in this course with me.

What lead you to this point?

I'd like you to write down the number ONE THING you want to gain from this course that would make it all worth it for you. You can write this in the space below; or, if you are happy to share, post a comment on our blog or Facebook page.

At the end of the course, we'll look back and make sure you got what you wanted.

The number ONE THING that I would like to gain from this course that would make it all worth it for me is:

Facts &
FOUNDATIONS
MODULE

Pre-Lesson
Basics

01.

The PRRE

The PRRE

About ten years or so ago now, I had been online researching how I could create nicer looking and better formatted word documents to assist me in what was then my small typing business, when I stumbled upon an interesting blog article discussing how people read documents – which I read because I thought the information could be useful at some point.

After a brief introduction to the article, the article-writer dived straight into wanting to do a fun little 'test' with those reading the article – which even after all this time, I still remember well.

The exercise involved finding a print out, where the text took up the whole page.

I didn't know where the writer was going with their article or exercise, but I decided to just follow the instructions without skipping ahead to find out what it was all leading to, like the writer was wanting.

I found a suitable looking page in my study, which as a discarded early draft of a resume I had recently typed up for a client, which I had not yet put through the paper shredder.

When I returned to the blog article, the author asked us to hold the page as though we were about to read it, and once we were doing this to then take notice of how and whereabouts I was holding the page.

The writer predicted that I was most likely to be holding the sheet of paper roughly at about the two-thirds down mark with the same hand that you use to write with, and that my thumbs would stick out into the middle of the page in a way that would prevent me from being able to read the last third of the page unless I shifted my grip.

I was indeed holding the sheet of paper in the exact manner the author described.

Being curious about what all this meant, I read on.

Now, even after all these years, I still remember the writer's point – good things have the great habit of just sticking with you like that, don't the y?

Turns out, that the area above my hold mark was the position the prime reader interest area; and the author's point being, where possible, this is the location where article writers should put their most interesting and important details.

That sounded reasonable enough. At first I didn't see how this new information could help me. But then I realised it might be beneficial to pass on to some of the students whose assignments I was typing up.

I had a small chuckle to myself that the resume I was holding fit into what the writer had been discussing even though the writer was talking more about writing essays and reports, and I even checked the final draft that I had given to the client, and was pleased to find it adhered to the rule too.

I made a mental note to remember this for future essays and assignment. And I thought I'd just mentally check the resumes I type up too, as I felt this was actually more important for resumes rather than just useful.

Not long after having read that article, maybe a week or two later, I was fortunate to gain another client wanting their resume typed up.

This new client was a real estate salesperson looking to change company's because he was experiencing pay issues.

Because his handwriting was really bad, the client provided me with copies of two or three different previous resume versions – 'none of which ever got [him] results', he advised. He felt that he did much better when he just met potential employers in person, but this time he didn't want his current boss to find out he was looking to change, so needed a resume to send out in response to advertisements and cold calls he made from home. A resume with better impact than the three he had.

He requested that I 'work out what needs to be put into the new resume' – meaning I shouldn't duplicate any information; just re-arrange and piece together the rest of the details so that it was logically presented and looked like a typical resume.

I settled down to make a start on completing the job just after he left, and I happened to look down and noticed that once again I was holding the multiple pages in the same position like that article I read had said – and was surprised that it still 'worked' even when holding more than one page.

But, during that glance at the topmost page of his resume, I noticed something else.

Apart from seeing my client's name and personal details typed in massive size (I'd say a font sized at 72 pt or more), there were no other details in that physical space.

And this got me thinking.

Was the clients' name the singlemost important detail? Or, were their better details that could occupy that space?

Now, I'd like to point out that back at that point in time I had no experience in hiring, recruitment or employment. Heck I wasn't even a real resume writer yet. This was only my third or fourth resume ever that I was typing up – and even then, I wasn't writing the resume. All I was doing was creating the electronic file from the clients' handwritten notes.

Although I had no experience, I suspected that any Real Estate Licensee-in-Charge would surely want to learn more than just an applicant's name. They would probably expect to see information related to the job in that space, so they could see he was highly experienced and had strong performance, and could therefore make a judgement that he might be suitable for them.

But this salespersons former resumes only held his name and contact details in that 'all important' topmost space. His name taking up almost half a page!

Where were all those fantastic, impressive, 'meaty' essentials that future employers would want to know about? They were all below my thumb line.

Was this the reason his resumes didn't get him results?

And I thought:

'This real estate agent is wasting his opportunity to sell his skills and abilities within the prime resume real estate zone'.

Yes. That physical space had suddenly metamorphosed into being more specific to this client and his employment as a real estate agent.

And from that moment onwards, regardless of the type of work sought, whenever I handled a person's resume, I mentally called that top two-third portion, 'the Prime Resume Real Estate' – or 'the PRRE', for short.

When the client came to collect his resume and USB and noticed how small I had made his name, he instructed me to resize those details as the only changes he wanted me to make. But, with my newfound knowledge (and confidence) I advised him that I didn't think it was in his best interest to waste the prime resume real estate in favour of only showcasing his name and contact details. I tentatively at first discussed that instead I believed he needed to ensure that only the information a real estate agency principal would want and expect to see would work best; and my belief that his name taking up more than half a page made his resume too much about him, and too little about what an employer would like to know about his skills and capabilities for the job.

He shocked me by responding with, *'Oh my goodness, you're right!'*

Now, the client still struggled with having his name and contact details remain so tiny by comparison to what it had been, and he acknowledged that it was because he had a dominant personality, and needed to tone himself back in his applications because a Licensee-in-Charge was likely to view him as a threat rather than an asset and good fit, until he proved himself in the role.

We compromised in the end. I made his name 24 point instead of 18. He got invitations to attend interviews from the very first application and soon moved on to a different agency – I know, because I saw his picture in the real estate section of our local newspaper.

So, there is an area on a printed resume page that is prime resume real estate.

And, just as the real estate industry expects to see quality houses in prime real estate areas, so too must jobseekers include quality details that interest and excite a hiring manager when they view the prime resume real estate area.

Everything above the thumb line on a printed page is the prime resume real estate. Everything covered up by your hands, or needs you to reposition them, falls outside of the PRRE.

Now, I can hear you asking already: what about electronic resumes?

Well, they have a prime viewing area too – only it is slightly less than for printed documents.

Because, when you open Microsoft Word (which is what most businesses use, even if you personally don't), on a typical computer screen the viewing area is only about half an A4 printed page length when viewed at normal size (the standard page size in Australia).

The File menu, Ribbon and Tabs take up a fair bit of the actual screen real estate – unless you switch across to full screen view mode, which not every reader does (and even then it only shows roughly two-thirds of an A4 page, when using a widescreen).

A hiring manager is able to gain an accurate feel for what the rest of the resume will be like just from that viewable half page worth, because our brain's visual processing power is so significantly faster than our text reading ability.

Throughout the tutorials in this book, I will refer to this prime resume real estate area as the PRRE.

02.

STRUCTURE of the Functional Resume

The STRUCTURE

Almost everything within our lives has a basic structure to it, from which individually stylised items can be developed or created.

For example, a cake consists of ingredients; a building has framework; the human body has its skeleton; an apple has its stem, core, flesh and skin.

It is your use of particular core structural ingredients which result in what type of cake you end up cooking, such as vanilla or chocolate, iced or un-iced, cream-filled or plain. Your cooking ability plays an important part in the end result as well of course, for example whether you overcook it, undercook it or it turns out as rich and moist perfection.

Buildings can have metal or wooden framework, and the quality of workmanship depends on the skill, experience and qualifications of the builder.

The human can be male or female, young or old, one ethnicity or another, in good health or poor, but at its most basic, we mostly all have a head, body and limbs as our basic framework.

That sort of thing.

Well, like in nature and in life, resumes have a structure too. In essence, a resume is simply a collection of different information sections and its accompanying details, which is presented in a particular way on a physical or electronic page.

And, like a basic cake recipe, it is often the ingredients used in addition to the core ingredients that change the variety being created, it is the resume sections you include or don't include and how you lay them out which determines whether you end up creating a functional, chronological, combination or even the dreaded mish-mash variety.

So what is the structure of the functional resume that we will be building?

The Functional resume format contains both what I consider to be essential and optional to include sections. The essential sections are the core ingredients, the optional sections are the embellishing extras.

For the functional format, there are just 5 core sections. These are:

1. Personal Details
2. Personal Profile
3. Core Skills
4. Work History, and
5. Educational Background

PARTS of the RESUME

PERSONAL DETAILS (1)
NAME SURNAME email@emailaddress.com 0411 223 344

JOB TITLE ~ JOB TITLE ~ JOB TITLE

Replace this text with your two- or three-line Career Goal or Dynamic Person Statement. This pitch needs to tie together your skills with what the employer is seeking. Keep it under 40 words if you can. A good practice is to tailor this to each application you submit.

CORE SKILLS (2)

- List the Skill Statement that you have identified as being the **most important** to employers in this space
- List your Skill Statements in order from most important at the top of the listing to least important at the bottom of the listing
- List your Skill Statements in order from most important at the top of the listing to least important at the bottom of the listing
- List your Skill Statements in order from most important at the top of the listing to least important at the bottom of the listing
- List your Skill Statements in order from most important at the top of the listing to least important at the bottom of the listing
- List the Skills Statement that you have identified as being the **least important** of all the required skills in this space

PERSONAL PROFILE (3)

- List the Personal Attribute Statement that you have identified as being the **most important** to employers in this space
- List your Personal Attribute Statements in order from most important at the top of the listing to least important at the bottom of the listing
- List the Personal Attribute Statement that you have identified as being the **least important** of all the required attributes in this space

INDUSTRY EXPERIENCE (4)

Position Title, Company Name	Start Date - Finish Date
Position Title, Company Name	Start Date - Finish Date
Position Title, Company Name	Start Date - Finish Date

EDUCATION, QUALIFICATIONS & LICENSING (5)

Name of Qualification	Year
Name of Licence or Permit	Currence Status

Every other section that you could possibly include in a resume is optional.

But when I say optional, I mean the section and its specifics must still be fully relevant and provide value to the type of work you seek to gain, otherwise the section should be kept out of your resume altogether. In other words, having discretion to include or not include must follow some rules.

If we were to look at the functional, chronological and combination resume formats lined up next to each other, we would see that each of the formats has its own particular core structure – although we can tell just by looking at them that they are a resume, they aren't the same.

You wouldn't be able to pick it up just by looking at the resumes side by side, but the key difference between the functional resume format compared to the chronological and combination formats lies within how we handle the Core Skills and Work History section specifics.

In the functional format, instead of keeping the gamut of information about one specific thing grouped together, they are intentionally divorced away from each other to form their own thing. That is, instead of listing all the skills, duties and accomplishments from each former employment and grouping them together as a lengthy, single listing with one full employment listed one after another to make Work History section, the core skills the person has becomes its own separate listing, and leaves the core employment basics for the work history section.

Some recruiters like this format because of this separation; others don't like it at all.

But, for jobseekers, particularly those with some employability weaknesses, it is this structural component which best enables them to use the separated out details to their application advantage; because it gives them the greatest opportunity to downplay weaknesses within their past work history to focus instead on what they can do, what they are competent at.

The functional resume, as a whole, is best when it is either a single filled page or two filled pages. So, depending on the job and how much skills and history you have then your goal will be to keep to that structure.

And as you will soon discover in the lessons when we drill down a bit further, both the order of the sections and the order of the specifics contained within the section are highly important and a key contributing factor as to whether the resume ends up as a quality resource or not.

In the next tutorial, we will look at the Strengths and Weaknesses of the Functional resume format, because it pays to know what advantages you need to leverage and what areas you need to strengthen. So, thank you for watching, and I'll see you in the next lesson.

03.

The BENEFITS (Strengths)

The BENEFITS (Strengths)

In our free course **'What TYPE of Resume do I Need?'** I discussed that the 3 resume formats each have their own particular areas of strength and weakness.

The key strength of the functional resume format is that its focus is on the job role (or in other words, the position vacant), rather than on the person per se.

I mean, by their very nature all resumes are about the person and are about the job, but I guess you could say the functional format is 'less interested' in that persons past work history and is 'more interested' in what specific skills they have and what they can do in the future.

It may be helpful to think of it like this:

In business you often hear advice similar to, *'Don't continually look over your shoulder and dwell on past successes, achievements or failures. Those things are all in the past and won't get you to your destination; they only led you to this current point. Instead, keep your eyes, goals and actions aimed firmly on the future. Because that's where your next success, achievement or failure lies, ready and waiting for you.'*

There is a second key strength of the functional resume format. And that is its 'tight control' of the sections and specifics to achieve an exact 1-page layout (or 2-page at most).

You've probably heard that our attention spans are getting shorter, that hiring managers only take between 2 to 30 seconds to review resumes, and that there is a trend of creating 1-page resumes. These are all true.

Well, what better way to achieve that than to use the functional resume format. If our attention spans have shortened, so too have hiring managers. If they don't have a long document filled with boring text, the chances are they are more likely to read the text rather than just skim read. A 1-page document will be more appealing to review than a longer one.

The great news for us then is that if they see our alignment to their needs, our suitability to the role, then our application will naturally survive the initial readthrough review, because they will be interested in us.

Too many jobseekers tell hiring managers too much about themselves, so they leave nothing for the hiring manager to want to know more about the person, they provide details which un-sells them and results in their application being rejected. The functional resume format forces you to think and decide carefully about what details to include and exclude. And when you leverage the formats strengths and minimise the weaknesses, the functional resume format is a powerful one.

04.

The DRAWBACKS (Weaknesses)

The DRAWBACKS (Weaknesses)

So what were the weaknesses for this resume format again?

In short from, they were:

- A risk of cramping too much information onto the page, which causes the resume's design to become cluttered and visually unattractive – which is a reading turn off

- Hiring managers can suspect that the person is using this format to disguise poor background, performance or skill level and that the information presented is incomplete - which is a hiring turn off

- Jobseekers often don't flesh out their section listings correctly, resulting in hiring managers not reading the details known to impress them, that are fully present and detailed in the chronological and combination formats – which is a rejection risk

As we go through this course, we will be working on the various ways and means to overcome these weaknesses, to turn reading turn offs into reading attractions, hiring turn offs into hiring interests, and boost our chance of progressing through the employers hiring process. So we won't go into all the weakness specifics that could easily depress or scare you.

Savvilicious! The employer just wants 1-page resumes --so I only need to create one using the Functional Format! My key details will already fall into the PRRE, naturally. So... all I need to do is pay careful attention to what details I include, and how I list them. Oh, this is easy as!

FORMULATE
MODULE

Develop Your
Resume
Content

LESSON 01.

PERSONAL DETAILS SECTION

TUTORIAL 01. PERSONAL DETAILS Section

This is video 1 of 4 for Lesson: Personal Details section.

When the Hiring Manager picks up a resume for the first time, they don't pay much attention (if any at all) to what the person's name and contact details are because they are more focused on getting their initial questions answered, and having those questions answered quickly.

But at some point, especially when the person has successfully demonstrated their potential suitability to the role, the hiring manager is going to want to know who the resume belongs to and how they can contact them – especially if they are interested in the person for the role.

When I did the first-round culling to reduce the hundreds of applications received down to a small, manageable shortlist our team would consider further, I was amazed to come across three mistakes so frequently.

These were, resumes:

- That did not have any contact information; ones
- With some of the crucial details missing; and
- Those that included far more personal information than was absolutely necessary

Let's discuss how each of those mistakes lead to the person's application being rejected.

No Contact Information or Some details missing

Because I was used to seeing resumes – the wow, the good, the bad and the downright ugly – it immediately stood out when an applicant failed to include their name or contact details as the first thing on their resume.

As soon as this was noticed, it then became a distraction in the shape of a curiosity.

Had the person missed including a crucial section of important information, or had they just positioned it elsewhere in the document?

For me personally, most of the time curiosity won out, and I would flip through however many pages the resume had, to resolve that question – which was a distraction from my reviewing intention. I had a few basic questions that I needed answering, but now I was trying to gain a different answer. If I had to flip through the pages, I was no longer skim-reading to work out if the person had the skills and experiences I was looking for, because my mind was focused on working out if the person had included their name and contact details elsewhere. And, I had now looked through the resume; and nothing special stood out to me, so even if I found the name and contact details, I just hadn't formed a good impression about the candidate – so having fully looked over the resume, could now reject it.

Actually, that distracting AWOL information curiosity was destined to result in a negative first impression regardless whether the applicant made it accidentally or intentionally.

Let's say the person had left the information out accidentally. As hiring managers we were left with being unable to contact them; so what point would there be to continue reviewing their person's suitability? None.

Let's say the person had, for whatever reason, repositioned the section to later pages. The result was they made important information too hard to find by placing it somewhere inconvenient and unexpected. As hiring managers we would ask, 'Why did you do this?' And because the person isn't around to answer this (also distracting) question, we would be forced to resolve the problem by making an assumption about possible reasons why the person did this.

Those assumptions would include had the person been lazy or in a rush? Were they possibly trying too hard to 'be different' or was this an application from unemployed person who is being forced to apply for a set number of jobs each week, who set out to sabotage any chance of their progressing forward within the hiring process? Or perhaps the person is just incompetent for some other reason and or just otherwise didn't understand the basics of creating a good resume and applying to jobs?

Can you see that each of those assumptions and questions causes the hiring manager to view this applicant from a negative mindset?

As hiring manager's, we didn't care to work out which of those scenarios or assumptions was true; we just decisively concluded that this applicant is both not the right candidate for our employer to hire and for us to work with; so reject their application on the spot without any further consideration.

Luckily, we didn't get too many resumes that didn't provide some or all of the candidates name or contact details.

Too Much Personal Information

But we did get an abundance of resumes that provided us with far more personal details than was absolutely necessary. And these resumes made my job of rejecting resumes just as easy as the last lot, because the extra details often enabled us to make decisions and assumptions – with all conclusions leading to 'not for us'.

In the next video we will explore 'What Personal Details are essential and how to avoid problems with them'.

TUTORIAL 02. PERSONAL DETAILS Section

This is video 2 of 4 for Lesson: Personal Details section.

The Two Essential Elements

So let's get clear. During the Hiring Phase, employers only need to know two (2) crucial personal details about applicants. These are the person's:

- Name, and their
- Contact details

(All other personal details fall into either the Optional or Exclude categories; but it is important to note that if you successfully gain the job, then additional details may need to be provided.)

The key to getting your job application to progress through the employers hiring process is to provide them with sufficient information that enables them to see your potential suitability, but to balance this with not including any information that leads to:

1. Their being able to make a 'No' decision without ever speaking to you first,
2. Forming a negative impression about you or your ability to do the job and do it well,
3. Enable them to discriminate against you, or
4. Enable anyone to misuse the information you have provided

The golden rule for including information in modern resumes is to think of your safety first. (This putting your own needs ahead of the employers only applies to the personal details section). Throughout the entire process of creating your resume, not just here in the Personal Details section, you should question every small personal detail and ask, 'Is this detail absolutely necessary (for the expression of interest stage)?' and 'Could this detail be misused?'

Let's now look at different Personal Details and which of the problems to avoid.

1. NAME

Employers also only need to know two (2) parts of a person's name. These are the persons:

- First name, and
- Surname

First Name

It is okay to apply to jobs using the name you commonly go by, if that is what you prefer.

For example, applying as Jo Surname, even though your official birth records name you as Joanne Surname.

Actually, by applying as Jo Surname rather than Joanne Surname, it could help prevent unscrupulous people misusing your personal information if you were to apply to a fake job vacancy.

Foreign Names

Also, jobseekers with long and unusual foreign names that are difficult to pronounce in their new country of residence often like use a shortened version, a nickname or common local equivalent, and this is perfectly acceptable too.

Middle Names

Just because your parents gave you a middle name or few, doesn't mean you need to include them on your resume. Actually, providing your middle names can be a scammer and identity thief's best friend, and is unnecessary additional information that takes up valuable space on your resume.

Surname

Some women adopt their de facto relationship surname, even when they haven't changed their official records and documentation. Again, it is perfectly okay to apply using the name you currently go by, but be prepared to clarify the situation later if you are offered the job.

Maiden Surname

Years ago (20 or more), women often included their maiden surname on their resume to explain why some documentation such as Educational certificates was in a different name to what is stated on the resume. But that practice has long since disappeared.

In modern resumes, this type of personal situation clarification is not only pre-maturely unnecessary during the application stage, it could lead to misuse by scammers and identity thieves, or a 'no decision' by the hiring manager for having demonstrated that you don't keep up to date of current practices!

It is important to remember here that you are not filling in an application form, creating a personal portfolio or creating a personal profile; you are creating a resume as part of your self-marketing materials to express your interest in opportunities that appeal to you.

Hiring Managers understand that women often take on the surname of their husband after they get married, and will probably (correctly) assume this to be the case when they see a female with 2 different surnames within their documentation. But the point here is that is too early in the hiring process to be providing documentary evidence of your education and other certificates and licensing.

Thankfully, this issue only comes up infrequently within the resumes I assess for clients.

2. CONTACT DETAILS

There are two methods that hiring managers' use to get in touch with jobseekers following reviewing their resume and job application. These methods are by:

- Telephone contact, or
- Email contact

Telephone contact

Most hiring manager's I know prefer initially contacting potentially suitable candidates by telephone rather than email, as it provides them with opportunity to ask the person a few questions before settling on whether to invite the person in for a face to face interview or not.

Our team preferred contacting potentially suitable candidates on their mobile phones rather than on a landline number.

Mobile phone

Many people have mobile phones, whether they utilise a pre-paid system or hold an account with their provider; and hiring managers prefer contacting jobseekers directly on their mobile phone number because they are more likely to:

1. Reach the intended person,
2. Can catch them straight away, or
3. Can leave a message knowing that the intended person is probably the (exclusive) account holder and therefore likely to receive the message; and
4. Often phone back missed calls to enquire about who and why the person was ringing.

Landline phones

Whereas, most landline numbers are there for the benefit of the entire household; so hiring managers cannot be sure the intended person will answer or will be available to take the call, which can leave the hiring manager to feel uncomfortable speaking with whoever does answer the phone because they cannot be sure they have the authority to tell them who they are and why they are calling in case it breaches the applicants privacy.

Creating and maintaining a good (first and lasting) impression

There are things you need to get right with regard to your telephone contact in order to create or maintain a good impression.

These are:

- Only listing one number on a resume
- Using correct style conventions
- Answering phone calls
- Voice messages and answering machines
- Returning missed phone calls

Only one number is needed

If the hiring manager wants to contact you, don't provide a couple of different numbers for them to try you on. They only need one phone number.

If they aren't successful in reaching you on first attempt, most hiring managers will try again later and or leave a message asking for the person to return their call.

For this reason, if you have both a landline and mobile phone number, then just include your mobile number on your resume.

Use Correct Style conventions

Each country has its own particular style convention for how to write out phone numbers.

In Australia, we layout a landline number like this:

   02 9600 3010

Which is: two digits space four digits space four digits; or, two digit area code followed by eight digit phone number (with space between for easier reading).

And we layout mobile phone numbers for local dialling like this:

0410 600 900

Which is: four digits space three digits space three digits; or, zero four (signals that the number is a mobile) one zero (the provider code) space three digits space three digits (the individuals personal number)

And we layout mobile phone numbers for international dialling like this:

+61 410 600 900

Which is: the plus symbol two digits space three digits space three digits space three digits; or +61 (international dialling code) four (the zero is dropped) one zero (the provider code) space three digits space three digits (the individuals personal number).

However, some people find it easier to remember their numbers in a way that makes it easier for them to remember. For example, for the mobile number 0411 119 922, the person might find it easier to remember and say it as:

04 11 11 99 22

Which is: two digits space two digits space two digits space two digits space two digits; or zero four pause eleven pause eleven pause ninety-nine pause twenty two

This may seem nitpicky to you, but when jobseekers don't use standard business style conventions it becomes immediately noticeable, especially by those that do use the correct style conventions. (And it is our job to point these types of things out to you so that you don't make these avoidable mistakes!)

When hiring managers see a number listed differently, it generally raises distracting questions in their mind (whether consciously or subconsciously): 'Has the person listed their number in this unusual manner because they are trying to be helpful? Or do they not understand standard business conventions exist, or do they know they exist but just don't care to follow them?'

The first thought gives the applicant the benefit of doubt, but as the person explores other possibilities, we head towards negative impression territory. Do they not understand standard business conventions? Hmmm, what else doesn't this person know if they don't understand basic written communication? Or do they know but just don't care to follow? Hmmm, if this is the case then the person is likely to not care about other things that are important to us. Bigger, more important things. Do we really want to risk hiring such a person?

On its own, writing a telephone number without using the correct style convention is unlikely to have too much of a negative impact on the person's application. The problem is that not using standard conventions often signals that information contained elsewhere within the resume will be at a poor level also, so the hiring manager will now be on the lookout for further evidence of unsuitability – and if they find even one small thing, that can be enough to end the applicant from progressing further.

And, if you are applying for Administration type work in particular, then this is even more important than ever, because you need to demonstrate your administration skills to employers at every opportunity. Administrative work candidates that don't use the correct style conventions are inadvertently revealing that they have poor written communication skills (in which case the hiring manager just laughs in disagreement 'This person doesn't know themselves very well' when they soon see 'Excellent written communication skills' in the Personal Profile or Core Skills section because the candidate has just proven the exact opposite – that they have less than excellent, and actually possess or have demonstrated sub-standard written communication skills).

Answering phone calls

Next, how you answer phone calls (especially from unknown numbers) matters!

You must answer in a professional business manner. That is, answer with a polite, welcoming and informative manner, saying something similar to *"Hello, [Your Name] speaking."*

What impression would you get if you were an employer phoning to offer a person an interview and the person answered with a grunting *'Hello?'* or worse, *'Who's this?'*

That 'Hello?' makes the answerer seem dopey or not quite with it, and the 'Who's this?' comes across as very rude and abrupt.

As the hiring manager with a position to fill, do you want to hire someone who is dopey or not quite with it? Not really, because they will be hard work, and probably problematic in the role. Do you want to hire someone who is rude and abrupt? No, let them go offend some other businesses' customers and staff – we certainly don't want them ruining what we've worked hard to build!

Hiring Managers won't tell you that they've had a change of mind in response to how you answered their call and will simply ask one or two 'pre-qualifying questions' and then say something like, 'Okay, that's all for now, we'll get back to you.' And then just never get back to you again.

(Though, it is important to note that many hiring managers do phone to ask pre-qualifying questions and from the responses you give will then progress you to their next stage – it's just that those that change their mind in response to how you answer the call and or the answers you give, will cut down on how many questions they ask compared to what they were going to, and will end the call quickly having already made their mind up).

Your voice mail or answering machine message

Voice mail and answering machine messages speak for you when you are unavailable at the time of the phone call. Just as how you answered in person is important and impacts upon the impression you make, so too do voice messages.

Whereas when the hiring manager phones and you answer they are forced into the situation of speaking to you for a short while until they can end the call, when they reach a voice mail or answering machine message that gives them a poor impression, they can simply not make any further attempt to contact you, and or hope that you are one of the many that do not return missed calls.

So again, a professional recording is in order. If it is a voice mail message for an account that is exclusively yours (like a mobile phone), then your message needs to specify your name so that the caller knows they have reached the right number (we all make dialling mistakes!) and therefore can have the confidence to leave a message. When it is a message for a household or group of people, then it would help if the message specifies the surname for the same reason.

What you don't want, while you are jobsearching, is for 'fun' recordings, like music and joke recordings. Leave those for exclusive benefit to family, friends and people who know you well, not potential future employers.

Return missed calls

Just because we carry portable phones around doesn't mean we are automatically available to answer them at the moment someone tries ringing us. Perhaps you are driving, so can't answer the call even though you hear it; or, you are like me and leave your mobile in your handbag and don't hear it ringing even though it is in the same room as you.

The point is, you will eventually learn that you had a missed call either from seeing a message on your phone stating you have a missed call, or an alert advising you that you have a new voice message; and as a jobseeker, it shows a basic level of business-mindedness and respect towards others when you return missed calls.

(As business-mindedness and respect towards others are highly valued by employers, it makes sense to implement them into your life and jobsearch!)

But you would be surprised at the number of jobseekers who don't return missed calls; and I don't understand why? For one thing, not all unknown callers are telemarketers, or debt collectors, or are calling for negative reasons; for another, employers aren't going to keep chasing you until they eventually get a hold of you. They'll try once or twice and then move on to an applicant that isn't as hard to get a hold of.

If they try and don't get a call back within an appropriate timeframe, they'll become unimpressed by your lack of professionalism and reject your application. An employer would rather play phone-tag a few times than to be (rudely) ignored.

In the next video, we'll cover the email.

TUTORIAL 03. PERSONAL DETAILS Section

This is video 3 of 4 for Lesson: Personal Details section.

Email contact

Being able to communicate with applicants by email is also important.

Firstly, some larger companies who receive large volumes of job applications whether the company is hiring or not are now bypassing contacting applicants by phone to instead invite them to attend an interview via email.

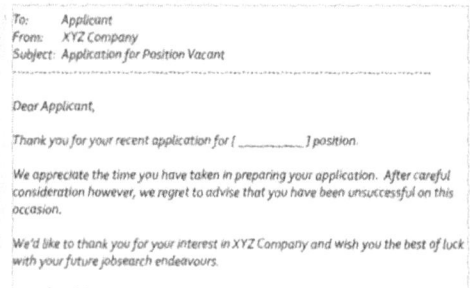

To: Applicant
From: XYZ Company
Subject: Application for Position Vacant

Dear Applicant,

Thank you for your recent application for [_____] position.

We appreciate the time you have taken in preparing your application. After careful consideration however, we regret to advise that you have been unsuccessful on this occasion.

We'd like to thank you for your interest in XYZ Company and wish you the best of luck with your future jobsearch endeavours.

Naturally, the applicants who check their email accounts regularly will learn about their having been successful in gaining an interview within sufficient time to make plans and arrangements so they can attend. Those who don't check their email accounts regularly, however, along with those who cannot attend at the specified date and time miss out on progressing further within that companies hiring process (unless the company has alternate dates and times available).

Furthermore, providing an email address enables the business to advise you when you have been unsuccessful in progressing through their hiring process (- yes, I know, not all businesses do this, but it allows the ones that do to do so), or send you confirmation details following a phone call.

So all in all, providing a telephone and email contact is standard in resume writing.

Now, there are things you need to get right with regard to your email too in order to create or maintain a good impression.

These are:

- Using a professional email address
- Easy to type addresses
- Not including age revealing numbers

Use a professional email address

Your email address can provide insight into your personality, attitudes and level of professionalism, so having a clear, non-offensive, non good impression reducing email address is imperative.

The most professional email address that you could use is:

yourname@provider.extension

If you don't have this structure of email address, then we encourage you to create one before you commence jobsearching. You could close it down and or stop using it once you have found a job if you want to.

The best place to get an appropriate email address is to use a web-email provider like Gmail, Live, or Yahoo (but I would recommend not using Hotmail because the extension is not professional sounding).

Use an address that is easy to type

Not everyone who works in an office or in an administrative based role possesses touch typing skills (we believe they should, because it increases their efficiency compared to hunt and peck typists, but that's another story and just our opinion).

Remember in an earlier video I discussed making life easier for the hiring manager? Well, making it easy for someone to type your email address without excessive switching from upper and lower case makes life easier for the hiring manager. Therefore, do not use too many full stops (periods), underscores (dashes that sit on the baseline), dashes, symbols, punctuation marks or fanciful combinations of letters and numbers which introduce difficulty with typing. For example, do not create or use an email address that looks like this:

^n.A.M_E@PrOV_idER*.com

...as it slows typing down significantly, while increasing the likelihood of making a mistake.

Don't include age-revealing numbers as part of your email address

If you open a free email account so that you can create a professional looking email address, you are likely to find that your name@provider.extension has already been taken; and the provider will offer up a few suggestions to try or use instead. These often contain numbers after the name but before the @ symbol – but this is not really ideal either, because it can lead to including age-revealing details.

You want your application to be reviewed and assessed on your merits to do the job and do it well, not assessed on how old you are (which is particularly important for younger and older workers).

What we suggest is that you use an alternative 'unique identifier' to enable you to get the email address you want. For example, I encourage my clients to use the initials 'JS' (which stands for job search, because other people haven't cottoned on to doing something like this... yet):

yourname.js@provider.extension

If you don't like the js, you could use something other than your year of birth, or how old you are – which make it easy for hiring managers to discriminate based on age without your ever knowing it. Whatever you choose should be neutral, unmeaningful or does not cause hiring decision problems.

In the next video, we will address the personal details that some jobseekers add to their resume but which should not be included at this stage or even at all.

TUTORIAL 04. PERSONAL DETAILS Section

This is video 4 of 4 for Lesson: Personal Details section.

Unnecessary Personal Details

So far, we have discussed that there are 3 pieces of personal details that belong in a resume, and how to make sure they give off the right impression.

Those 3 details are:

- Your name
- Your email address, and
- Your contact number

Now we need to discuss what personal details are unnecessary and therefore unadvisable for inclusion on your resume (and applications).

The personal details that are not necessary during the application stage (but which the employer will require to hold on file later on) include:

- Residential address
- Age
- Date of Birth
- Tax File Number
- Bank Account details
- Salary expectations (and only if asked)

(Though it is important to note that some large companies request this information in application forms they get you to fill out as part of their hiring process. Before you hand over these details, ensure the company is well known and reputable. If you have any doubts about the company and their need for the last three personal details in particular so early within the hiring process, then err on the side of caution and either wait until you are being offered the role or seek out assistance from a parent or other authority so you don't fall victim to a scam or identity thief).

The personal details that should never be included in a resume at all or at any stage of the hiring process include:

- Sexual preference
- Problematic personal situations like your financial situation

The personal details that you make want or need to discuss depending on the job and your circumstance includes:

- Disability, injuries and health conditions
- Religious preference
- Political preference
- Marital status
- Parental / Carer status
- Criminal history

As discussed back in Video 2, including these types of personal details can have serious detriment to your application, because they enable the hiring manager to:

1. Make a 'No' decision without ever speaking to you first,
2. Make a negative judgement about you, your circumstance or your ability to do the job and do it well,
3. (Consciously or unconsciously) discriminate against you
4. And, the additional details expose you to risk of unscrupulous people misusing the information you have provided for their own hidden agendas and personal gains (often at an expense for you).

Activity Time!

Yay! You have reached the first of a number of student activities for the course.

The first is the Quiz below, followed by the first Workbook activity.

1. Quiz – Email Address suitability

Having now read the learning materials for the Personal Details section, is the email address you intend listing on your resume suitable for jobsearch purposes?

- Yes
- No

2. Workbook Activity

Before you move to the next lesson, we want you to take action towards developing your unique resume content; as we believe you will feel less stress about the process if you take small frequent steps at the end of each chunk of learning rather than leaving it all for the end.

Instructions

On page towards the back of the workbook, you will find a section entitled **"Functional Resume Master Worksheet"**.

In the space provided for "Personal Details", please now fill in your:

- name
- email address, and
- mobile phone number

*Note. Again, if you do not already have a suitable email address, then you will need to create one. We highly recommend that you go and do this now, and then come back. That way, you will be able to finish the entire Student Activity completely and not be left with missing details to fill in later on.

LESSON 02.

TERMINOLOGIES CLARIFIED

TUTORIAL 01. TERMINOLOGIES Clarified

Hi, thanks for joining me again. Before we move to the next section that needs to be included in a Functional Resume, I feel it is necessary for me to clarify some of the terminology that I will use throughout the rest of the course – in particular for lessons 3 to 7.

So Lesson 2 is a short supplementary lesson where I will clarify what I mean by the words:

- skills
- skill categories
- skill statements
- personal attributes, and
- personal attribute statements

... and discuss the differences between them. So let's get started.

The Difference between Skills, Skill Categories, Skill Statements, Personal Attributes and Personal Attribute Statements

I'll start with Skills.

Skills are...particular tasks that you can do well, and that other may not be able to do (at all, or very well).

Examples

- Driving
- Washing
- Calculating
- Data entry
- Writing

Skill Categories are... A collection of related-skills combined into a single 'umbrella-termed' grouping.

An example of a Skill Category is: 'Computer Skills'.

Specific computer skills might include:

- Typing
- Data entry
- Emailing
- Web-publishing

- Document formatting

Skill Statements are... Information-packed sentences, which provide specific details showing a particular skill 'in action'.

Examples

- Answer 100 telephone calls per day using PABX system (answering phones)
- Provide relevant product information to facilitates customers purchasing of Manchester-department products (product knowledge or sales skills)

Personal Attributes are... A quality (or characteristic) of the person.

Examples

- Punctual
- Honest
- Friendly

Personal attributes statements are...information-packed sentences, which provide specific details that demonstrate the personal attribute (quality or characteristic) in action.

Examples

- Arrive on time to open branch for staff to set up and prepare for day's trading.
- Pitch in to serve customers during high volume periods

In other words...

- A skill is about what the person can do
- A personal attribute is about what the person is like
- A skill category is a grouping of related skills
- A skill statement is an evidence-based sentence that demonstrates the skill in action
- An attribute statement is an evidence-based sentence that demonstrates the persons qualities in action

The reason for understanding the differences is:

1. Every person has skills and personal attributes
2. Job advertisements often list skill categories rather than individual skills
3. And, probably the most important of all, jobseekers need to write Skill and Personal Attribute Statements when creating their resume.

LESSON 03.

CAREER OBJECTIVE SECTION

LESSON INTRO

Welcome to Lesson 03 Career Objectives in the Develop Your Resume Content module.

The Career Objective section is the first of the Summary Information that we will include in our Functional Resume.

In the video tutorials, we will look at four key areas related to career objectives:

1. Whether the Career Objective section is a MUST-HAVE, a MUST-NOT-HAVE or is simply an Optional section for you to decide whether you want to include the section or not
2. What a standard Career Objective looks like
3. What alternatives - if any - you can use, and
4. Then I'll show you exactly how to write statement so that it sets a positive tone and maybe even gives the hiring manager a little thrill of excitement or enthusiasm to read what else is in your resume.

So, I'll see you in the tutorials!

TUTORIAL 01. CAREER OBJECTIVE Section

This is video 1 of 5 for Lesson: Career Objective section.

Hello again.

In this first tutorial of Lesson 03 the Career Objective section, we'll explore whether a Career Objective is a compulsory to include section or not in a Functional Format Resume.

So, let's get straight into it, shall we?

Is a Career Objective section a MUST-HAVE, a MUST-NOT-HAVE or is it fully OPTIONAL?

I'll answer this upfront: Including a Career Objective section is *fully optional* for the Functional Format resume.

The reason for this is:

Not all hiring managers will read them – because often the information in a typical or standard Career Objective focuses on what the jobseeker wants or aims to achieve.

And well, to put it bluntly, hiring managers don't actually care about what the jobseeker wants – especially not at this early hiring stage when they don't even know if they will like you as a potential candidate or not – so the information is immediately BORING and UNMEANINGFUL to them.

Actually, some hiring managers HATE Career Objectives with a passion, viewing them negatively as nothing more than wandering 'Go Nowhere' self-focused 'Me, Me, Me...' dribble, that don't provide any VALUE or LEAD SOMEWHERE SPECIFIC.

I've observed that the higher up the career ladder a person gets, the more expected Career Objectives seem to become; so the trick for jobseekers who include the section is to provide relevant and interesting details that cause hiring managers to become impressed by the candidate – because, a Career Objective sets the tone and expectation level for the rest of the resume.

In other words, get the section and details right, and hiring managers are likely to be left with a positive impression and therefore likely to look forward to reviewing the remainder of the resume – perhaps enough to progress the application through to the next stage of secondary reviews; but get it wrong, and they won't be keen to even lookover the rest of the resume at all, and they are more likely to toss the application to their rejection pile (or close the electronic file down, and transfer it to their 'not for us' folder) - opportunity over for that person.

Now, you have chosen the functional resume format, probably because you aren't likely to be applying for higher level roles. So for you, the decision becomes 'Do I include a section that potentially won't be read or could create the wrong impression, or can I (or should I) leave it out altogether?

That choice is fully up to you.

I don't add Career Objective statements to many of the resumes I create for clients, unless they are indeed going for higher positions. But I've had a few jobseekers say to me, and I agree with their consensus that not having the section can make the resume look sparse on details, or worse, make the resume look like it is missing something (which, in all fairness, it technically is).

But before you make up your mind on whether you will include the section or not, let's look at what a typical career objective statement looks like, to see why so many hiring managers don't bother reading them – and then I'll show you how to write interesting statements so you can impress the ones that do read them, which will help you decide if you want to include this section in your functional resume.

So, what does a typical Career Objective look like?

The best way to understand what a typical career objective looks like is with an example. I've gone through some very old resumes that clients have sent me, and come up with a couple that represents the typical career objective that are the reason hiring managers have become so turned off by this section.

Here's the first example:

> "To obtain a role which will allow me to use my experience and make a valuable contribution to the business."

Now, you may be thinking, that doesn't sound bad. Why wouldn't hiring managers like reading this? The answer is: for starters, it doesn't set the person apart; and secondly, what is that statement really saying? Not much.

Every single jobseeker could write that (and often do).

You have to consider, when you are a hiring manager receiving hundreds and thousands of resumes, with the same type of bland and uninteresting statement; and you are busy and have a lot of resumes to go through, you would look for opportunities that enable you to cut down how long it takes to sort through applications – and reading statements that you know aren't going to do anything for you become the first item you can easily skip.

We need to analyse that career objective, from the hiring managers' or employers perspective for those that aren't yet so jaded that they still do read them – a step, by the way, that we should always take within the resume writing process – considering things from the hiring manager's perspective.

With our hiring manager hat on, that objective leaves us with questions – that distract us from our main purpose in why we are reviewing the resume:

"To obtain a role which will allow me to use my experience ..."

- **"What experience does this person have?"**

At this point, our hiring manager knows nothing about the person except that they have mentally noted that their personal details section is present – and therefore they will be able to contact them later if they are interested in them for the role.

The answer to that 'What experience? question becomes: Oh, I have to read through the resume and work this out.

"... and make a valuable contribution to the business."

- ***"How, exactly, will you make a valuable contribution to our business? I haven't learned a thing about you yet, and your promising valuable contribution! Valuable contribution would be telling me what skills and experiences you have!"***

Let me point a few things out here.

Our hiring manager picked up the resume to start learning a bit about you so that they can decide if you seem to have what they are looking for. But instead of the resume starting to answer a hiring managers initial basic hiring questions they have now formulated two inconsequential questions that have distracted them from their main purpose and are, frankly, irrelevant.

Furthermore, those two inconsequential questions aren't being adequately answered either! They provoke sarcastic and negatively-retorting thoughts.

Hiring Managers don't have time to work out what skills and experiences the person has that might enable them to provide a valuable contribution in the role. The jobseeker needs to show and tell the hiring manager what their skills and relevant experiences are, so the hiring manager can see that the person will provide a valuable contribution to their business needs, above all the other applicants who have applied.

Next, without any specific details of substance that career objective statement is just a baseless hollow claim by the jobseeker. A fluff statement.

Fluffy hollow claims are not only boring and unmeaningful to the recipient, but such statements in a resume become a waste of valuable prime resume real estate space; and a waste of the decision maker's time forcing them to read such meandering dribble.

Consider this: Boxer, Mohammed Ali, once famously publicly declared in the hype before a world title fight against Sonny Liston: "I am the greatest!" People didn't believe him because he claimed this about himself, actually, they thought he was arrogant for having stated this – no, they believed him because he proved from winning fifteen fights before this that he was a good boxer to even be facing Sonny Liston. And his subsequent surprise seventh round winning of the world title shortly after proclaiming to the world that he is the greatest, cemented the public's opinion that he wasn't just a good boxer, he was indeed the greatest.

He had set the tone of what the public could expect from his upcoming performance... and he delivered on that promise. If he hadn't the public would have rejected any and all future claims of greatness Mr Ali might make.

The career objective, as the first piece of reading a hiring manager will find, sets the tone and quality-level for what they can expect from elsewhere within the document.

A bland and meaningless statement will inevitably leave the hiring manager with a poor impression, right from the get-go. And of course, no hiring manager is going to progress any application through to their next stages when any particular application has caused them to view that candidate negatively ... and so quickly!

If they don't see anything that changes their mind, they can conscionably reject the application.

Actually, it gives them an excuse to skim the rest of the PRRE for the sole purpose of satisfying that it is okay to reject it without any deeper-level review and without any feelings of possible guilt. Because yes, hiring managers are human. And sometimes it hits you that you are receiving applications from real people – real people who are desperately wanting and needing a break, hoping you'll choose them. Doing the initial culling reviews can be a hard task, because you know you're going to disappoint way more people than you'll ever please with a phone call.

Okay, let's try another example, so you can see how non-impressing such statements can be now that you are seeing things more from the hiring manager's perspective:

"To find a suitable job that fits my past experiences, skills and previous jobs."

Do you see how uninteresting, how unmeaningful, how blandly horrible that objective is?

I repeat: Employers and hiring managers DON'T CARE that you want to find a job, let alone whether it will be suitable for you. They care about finding a person who will be suitable to fill their vacancy. Ideally, the person they find the most suitable will find the role suitable in return.

Again, let me point out a few home truths here.

Some really skilled hiring managers will read the career objective like that and instantly know that the person isn't for them, and then not even bother reading until the end.

Why? Look at the logical side.

Firstly, EVERY job applicant who sends in a job application to any vacancy wants to find a suitable job.

Secondly, EVERY job applicant wants to find a role where their skills, experiences, and capabilities fit and benefit THEM in some way.

This is a given.

Employers, as we know, care about finding the most suitable person who fits their vacancy needs.

Too many jobseekers treat, and that type of career objective show that, sending an application with the misguided expectation that an employer is expected to review the person's application and find a place where they can slot the person in if they are a good fit for the company but not this particular role.

It is not up to the hiring manager to make a thorough and in-depth assess of a person's skill set and history and decide if they might fit. It is your job, as a candidate, to demonstrate how your skills, experiences and capabilities make you possibly suitable to that one role and vacancy that they have in your application materials. That is, your resume and cover letter.

Stating your own needs won't instil anyone with confidence, let alone a hiring manager, that you want to do the type of work with which they happen to have vacancy for; doing this only makes the applicant look too self-absorbed, as 'what I bring to the party' is their only offering – which just demonstrates that the person was too lazy to spend time to demonstrate on paper the how and why that results in possible suitability.

Whether it is in business or personal context, you should know that one-sided relationships never last in the long term; sooner or later, the other party gets resentful and fed up with the selfish party only looking after numero uno; and savvy hiring managers know full well the consequences in hiring the wrong person, and is on the lookout for candidates who are only 'in it for what I can get out of it' and will gladly and hastily reject applications from those who show this aspect to their personality.

So, if you are going to include a career objective in your functional resume – which we've discussed is fully up to you – then you must provide specific details that make the statement interesting to read and value-packed for the employer.

In other words, you will need to intentionally avoid discussing what YOU want, to instead write a sentence that focuses on what THEY want, need, expect or might be interested in.

You may now find yourself thinking, I think there may be alternatives to writing a typical career objective. And if you are thinking this, then you'd be right.

In the next tutorial, we'll look at fantastic two alternatives that professional resume writers often use in place of a career objective, for those of you who would like to keep the career objective section in your resume but appreciate the need to make a positive impact rather than a poor one.

So, I'll see you in the next tutorial.

TUTORIAL 02. CAREER OBJECTIVE Section

This is video 2 of 5 for Lesson: Career Objective section.

Hello again.

In this second tutorial of Lesson 03 the Career Objective section, we'll explore the alternatives to writing a Career Objective for those of you who would like to keep the section in your Functional Format Resume, and for those of you trying to decide what you should do.

So, what are the alternatives to writing a standard career objective statement?

There are two alternatives. And both are much better options than the example career objectives we discussed in the last tutorial.

The first is what is known as a **Goal Statement**.

And the second is what I have called a Dynamic Person Statement, because I don't know of anyone else that uses this type of statement, let alone enough for it to have a title already.

Let's have a look at both.

a. Goal Statement

The title of this statement suggests exactly what this option is about. That you need to write a clear and concisely worded statement about what your GOAL is for yourself within the job, along with the benefits you bring to that type of role.

That means, you must know quite clearly the job role you are applying for, and what the position entails, so that you can highlight your greatest strengths for that type of job and create a mental picture for the hiring manager to envisage you in that role.

Again, the best way to demonstrate what I am talking about is to use an example:

"My goal is to use my warehouse knowledge and experience in safe working practices, so that I transport goods with a minimum of spoilage."

Can you see already how much better this sentence is compared to the career objectives from the last tutorial? This statement is both targeted and relevant to the position being sought.

It doesn't take a genius to work out that the writer is clearly applying for a role in the warehousing industry. My guess is that he or she was going for a FORKLIFT DRIVER …or similar role. Straightaway, this person's 'career objective' provides instant value and was more interesting to read than those earlier examples.

Aside from stating 'my goal is…' let's break down what this applicant's employment goal is?

Can you pick it? It is: To transport goods safely.

Would this statement provide any value for an employer who is seeking to fill a Forklift Driver or other warehouse position? Most definitely, yes. The goal statement demonstrates (without the candidate needing to specify it overtly) that the candidate understands the needs and expectations of the role, which fully aligns him to what employers of this job role want, need and expects from potentially suitable candidates.

The tone has been set – this resume is from an applicant with experience in a warehouse environment. If I was the hiring manager, I would experience the first small thrill of excitement that I may have just won a mini- job application lottery. A 'Yes, this is what I'm looking for!' moment.

And naturally, I'd be keen to review the rest of this resume, because it is off to a very strong and positive start, so I could see if there are other things about this applicant that would make him (or her) possibly suitable and worthy of considering further.

The hiring manager would move on to review the rest of the resume. But we'll stay looking at why they would have gained that small thrill of excitement.

Without even asking the question, the hiring manager would gain the following answers:

1. **Do they have experience?** Yes. '… use my warehouse knowledge and experience…' immediately and clearly resolves the answer to their most fundamental initial question.

2. **What benefit is this applicant promising to bring to our business?** Minimum of spoilage – or waste – from accidental damage. Yes! Of course an employer seeking to hire a Forklift Driver would be highly interested in any candidate who aspires to do the job safely and do a good job which working safely would entail, so that our organisation isn't losing money through damaged goods or workplace accidents.

Although hiring managers wouldn't ask themselves this question, that goal statement does answer one other question that I encourage you to consider as fundamentally important.

Does the statement paint a mental picture that enables the reader (me, the hiring manager) to see the person performing in this type of role? And my answer is: You bet it does.

Instead of no mental picture at all, or a wrong one, the moment I personally read the words 'warehouse' I heard the imaginary sound of a beeping reversing signal, and I mentally pictured, in full colour, a male sitting in the cabin of a forklift, looking over his shoulder as he backed his load away from its shelves, driving the forklift in a non-reckless manner. The man that sprung into my mind was wearing fluoro safety vest, a white hard hat though I could still see that he was a dark haired man, and that he was wearing matt black steel cap boots.

Did I get a mental picture like this for either of the typical career objective statements from earlier? No. My mind remained image free. And if images did try to form, they remained foggy and non-distinct.

Did you gain a mental image?

Even if you don't form fully colourful mental images quite as vividly as I do, most readers get a brief mental image flash before them in their minds eye, even if they don't realise it – and importantly, it means so too do hiring managers. That's the power certain words can have on people. I'm lucky in that I create strong visual imagery.

But even if I didn't form a mental picture in my mind, I'll be honest: I would still find that goal statement more positive than those typical career objectives. In a sea of resumes where every other candidate writes a typical career objective that is self-focused, this sole person who has focused on the needs of the job would be like a refreshing breath of clean air; and could very likely be the tipping point to why this candidate singularly stands out and impresses where no others come remotely close

Of course, this person might also not be the one who is eventually offered the job or gets an interview, but I can tell you one thing: their application will be treated seriously and be given full and proper consideration. Therefore, it most like that the hiring manager will skim read the resume of the resume and possibly put it off to one side for a more thorough and in-depth consideration later on – and thus giving him or her the 'fair chance' towards gaining this job that applicants want to gain. Which, even though our previous two candidates won't see it this way, but who were also given a 'fair chance', but failed at hitting the mark because of their content choices.

Now, in the next tutorial I will teach you how to write a strong and compelling goal statement like this, but for now, let's move on and look at the Dynamic Person statement

b. Dynamic Person Statement

The best way I can describe what a dynamic person statement is, is that it is like a testimonial or recommendation you make about another person that you have complete faith in. Only, instead of telling people how wonderful someone else is, you are writing a statement and telling the reader, using third-person viewpoint, how great (or dynamic) YOU are – and minus all the previous "*me*-related" wording.

An example is:

"*A talented Salesperson with proven history in following up leads and referrals, and converting discussions into opportunities leading to sales transactions.*"

I love writing and reading dynamic person statements, because there is something really appealing about someone who:

1. Knows themself really well,
2. Has confidence in themself and their abilities, and
3. Is happy to talk about their strengths and capabilities in a way that doesn't come across as arrogant or bragging.

This person, in the comfort of their own home or non-work environment away from his or her colleagues, might be able to say to family members or close friends how they see their own honest achievement, correct behaviour or attitude comparing themself to co-workers who don't do the same thing, 'I'm the only one at work who follows up on all leads and referrals that are given to me', and 'I seem to have a great knack for persuading people to buy our companies products and services – either on-the-spot or within the next few days.'

I've found that when we tell our family and friends things like this, it is usually because we are more expressing our curiosity as to why those other people don't do the same thing, rather than as outright criticism of those other peoples actions (or non-actions as the case is here) or from boastfulness. Because our family and close friends will be the first people to let us know when they think we hold the wrong attitude.

What I love about expressing those types of curiosities is that they provide great fodder for converting into dynamic person statements – because face it, if no one is complimenting us on a job well done, then we should tell people what we get right.

And, as you already understand, what we use as our opening statement sets negative tone and quality level as positive or negative for what the person will find for the rest of the document.

So, by writing as though we are talking about someone else (which is what third person viewpoint writing is about), we remove the 'He (or she) is a bit full of him or herself' sides to and judgements made about our discussing our own personal strengths, behaviours and achievements.

You may be wondering: Why does writing a dynamic person statement work better than a career objective statement? And the answer is simple: Because again, the person is showing what they can do and the benefits they bring to the workplace or role. They are being direct and specific, not vague, wishy-washy or talking in riddles.

Let's look at things from the hiring manager's perspective again.

Remember that main initial question employers have when they review an application: does this person have experience?

"...A talented Salesperson with proven history..." We can mentally tick that checkbox, can't we?

What about the second question: **what benefit is this applicant promising to bring to our business?**

What would YOU want and expect of a Salesperson? I know I'd want them to follow up on every possible lead and referrals, and to gently guide all interested potential customers ultimately towards purchasing our products or services – which is the whole purpose of such a sales person role. So, they are once again demonstrating that they know the role and what is involved, and showing the benefit that they hold the same result outcome that we, the employer, want.

But remember my other fundamentally important question that I encouraged you to always consider:

Does it create a mental picture of the person in the role?

"A talented Salesperson with proven history in following up leads and referrals..."

Yes, it does.

Straightaway, when I read the words 'following up leads...' I mentally saw the mental image of a male wearing a swanky business suit sitting at a desk, non-significantly reach forward and pick up the office telephone handset and start punching in numbers to make a call. And when moments later I read the words 'sales transaction' for a brief moment I saw a dollar sign and heard an accompanying ca-ching sound flash before my mind's eye, before I mentally pictured the scene of my salesman hanging up the phone, leaning back in his office chair with a pleased smile on his face and doing a small discrete fist pump to express how happy he is with how that call panned out. And I just knew that he had converted that discussion into a sale – for my company.

Hopefully by now you can see that when a hiring manager reads a dynamic person statement like this, it grabs their attention, and causes them to become interested in the candidate.

This applicant is clearly a Salesperson, and employers looking for a salesperson – now that they have had their main question 'do they have experience?' answered – would want to know the next main thing that concerns them for a person holding a Sales role: 'Just how successful they are at converting leads into sales?'

Because as we discussed a few minutes ago, the whole purpose of a business hiring salespeople is for them to generate revenue and build customer relationships so the business successfully generates profits for now, and into the future.

At this point, our hiring manager wanting to know how successful they are means one thing: they are interested in this candidate.

An assumption will take place: the person's Core Skills section is the most likely place that they will find specifics about their level of achievement in converting leads into sales. So, rather than waste time learning what skills this person has – because we already know they have relevant ones now – we may be tempted to skip straight past the Personal Profile section to go in search of those quantifiable amounts and specific results.

This applicant has no idea how close they are to either being invited in to a job interview, or ruining the fantastic first impression they have created!

I can't make it any clearer:

Employers wanting to skip ahead to look for specific details means you have successfully grabbed their attention and built their initial hiring interest – and that's our entire goal of a resume, isn't it – so this applicant must back their successful start up by providing the supportive particulars that keep the hiring manager interested.

When you get a hiring manager this excited, they will feel more disappointed if you let them down now.

RECAP
So, let's review what we've learned so far:

Firstly, we've discussed that a Career Objective type section is completely optional, and secondly, there are two better alternatives that you should use over a typical career objective, and these are goal or dynamic-person statements.

In the next tutorial, I will teach you how to write quality goal and dynamic person statements. So, I look forward to seeing you in the next tutorial.

TUTORIAL 03. CAREER OBJECTIVE Section

This is video 3 of 5 for Lesson: Career Objective section.

Hello again.

I'm really glad that you are sticking with me. In this tutorial which is Lesson 03 Tutorial 03 in the Develop Your Resume Content module, I'm going to teach you how to write a quality 'Career Objective' section statement.

I say Career Objective using air quotes here, because as I've discussed, I have no intention of teaching how to write a boring, typical career objectives.

I'm going to teach you to write goal statements and dynamic person statements that will make you stand out in a more positive way.

You ready to get started? I know I am.

4. How to Write a Quality "Career Objective" section statement.

It is only really possible to write unique and compelling value-driven statements when you know two (2) specific things:

1. The Job, and
2. Yourself.

You need to know your job and personal strengths and where your abilities lie for this specific type of job role, and therefore you need to know what the job role really entails, either through having worked in the industry or similar position previously, or from having undertaken thorough research into the industry, employers and job role if you don't have first-hand experience.

We'll decide later if you should choose a goal statement or a dynamic person statement if you are feeling inspired to include the section.

But, first I'll teach you how to write goal statements – and will send you off to go and complete the activities in your Student Workbook – and then when you return, I'll teach you how to write dynamic person statements – and will send you off again to go and complete the activities in your Student Workbook – and when you return to this lesson again, I'll get you to decide if you want to write a goal statement or dynamic person statement for your functional resume.

How to Write Goal Statements – Part 01

The key to a good goal statement is to know the core purpose of the job role

In the last tutorial, I pointed out that the core purpose of a salesperson is to connect with potential customers and drive them towards a purchase transaction.

So a key task or responsibility to achieve that core purpose would be for them to convert 'leads' (either self-sourced or provided to them) into a paying customer (bringing about a sale).

Every job has a core purpose. That core purpose will be different for every job. So, I want you to think about the type of job that you seek to gain, and work out what the core purpose of that role is.

I'll give you another example to help you identify a jobs core purpose.

When I was a Disability Employment Consultant, the core purpose of the job for the consultant was to manage a caseload of unemployed people and drive them to overcome their disability, injury or temporary health condition and barriers to employment so that they found suitable work and met their social security requirements. A key task within the role was to diarise and report upon the jobseekers compliance with looking for work and addressing their barriers, and to provide resume and jobsearch assistance to help them gain a job that will sustain them.

But, for the employers of consultants, the core purpose of the role was for the consultant to achieve one key thing: which was outcomes. Outcomes meant the candidate reached certain milestones within specific times:

It meant that the jobseeker:

- Gained a suitable and sustainable job,
- Which resulted in their meeting specific hours and weekly income levels (called benchmark requirements), and then
- Maintained working at or above their minimum benchmark requirement uninterruptedly over two specific periods, being
- 13 weeks (which is 3 months) and 26 weeks (which is 6 months) which when successfully attained, resulted in that person becoming an Independent Worker (that no longer needed to be monitored or compliance checked).

Resolving a barrier, or creating a resume for the client weren't outcomes; these types of tasks just paved the way to make it smoother and easier for the client to achieve an employment outcome.

Employers, and consultants, put strategies in place to help jobseekers achieve their employment goals and milestones so that they exited our caseload as an Independent Worker. But, as you can see, the core purpose really comes down to which perspective you are viewing it from.

An outcome for the jobseeker resulted in an outcome for the consultant, which in turn resulted in an outcome for the business, which in turn also became an outcome for the government who had contracted employers to deliver services for them.

So, as I have encouraged you elsewhere within this course, put yourself into looking at things from an employer's perspective, as this could make all the difference between you targeting what every other applicant targets versus getting at the heart of what will concern the employer.

At this point, I want you to pause or stop this video, so that you can go and complete the first Student Workbook activity for this lesson: WB02 – Core Purpose of the Job. Please take your time when completing activities, and don't rush. When you are ready, please rejoin me.

WB02. CORE PURPOSE OF THE JOB
Read the Video Tutorial transcript: Write a Goal Statement (above), and then answer the following questions.

2.1	What job role are you seeking to gain?	
2.2	What is the core purpose of that job role?	
2.3	What do you want to achieve when you get this type of job?	
2.4	Does this align well with what employers of this job role want, need or expect?	☐ Yes ☐ No

	Why / why not?	

Welcome back. How did you go answering those questions?

If you had any problems in completing that exercise, and you don't have family or friends that can help you work it out without my assistance, then please contact me and I'll do my best to get back to you as soon as possible so I can steer you in the right direction on what the core purpose of your particular job type might be.

Now that you've done that activity, we'll move on to learning how to write statements that we can use for a career objective section. The first statement we'll look at is goal statements.

How to Write Goal Statements – Part 02

In preparation for writing this course, I spent a considerable amount of time looking over past resumes I've received and printed out with my trusty highlighters in hand with the aim of finding and marking common threads, if any. As suspected when I started this activity, I found that the best of statements could be broken down into key segments. From this, I went on and developed a simple formula that I could use to help clients write a unique and compelling sentence without making it too obvious that a formula had been used.

Once I had my formula, I then compared it against many of the samples career objective type statements I found in a couple resume writing books that I own, and consistently found that while the formula was not exactly the same, each of the statements in the samples did indeed adhere to similar structures very close to the formula I had come up with.

So, to help you get started with writing a statement that will be far better than a typical career objective, I'll now share my formula with you. It is this:

- My goal is to use my – blank
- To – blank
- So that – blank

> **My goal is to use my** ____[*fill in the blank with a*]____[*skill, experience, knowledge, talent, competency, personal attribute etc*] **to** ____[*fill in the blank, this time, answering to*] ____ [*do what?*] **so that** ____[*fill in the blank, so that*]_____ [*you achieve what benefit?*].

Now let's look at how we might fill in those blanks.

With **the first blank**, you will write down a claim-based word, such as:

- skill
- experience
- knowledge
- talent
- competence
- attribute
- etc

So the sentence looks like this:

- My goal is to use my skill
- My goal is to use my experience
- My goal is to use my knowledge
- My goal is to use my talent
- My goal is to use my competency
- My goal is to use my ... fill in a word of your choice

The **second blank** needs to answer the question of '*do what?*' – which is the employer interest generating component.

And the **last blank** needs to answer the question of '*so that you achieve what benefit?*' – which is demonstrates the value you would bring to the role.

The best way to show you what to write in the second and third blank, of course, will be with an example.

Now, in the last tutorial I provided you with a dynamic person statement for a salesperson. So let's say he now wants to write a goal statement. Using the formula, we will take what we know about our salesperson, and write a goal statement for him.

Salesperson's Goal Statement

The first step, as we already discussed is to consider the core purpose of the type of work he seeks to gain.

Core purpose

The core purpose for a salesperson role – regardless of which specific industry the job role is – would be to connect with potential customers and drive them towards a purchase transaction.

Therefore, if our salesperson worked in the:

- **Real estate industry**, he would be aiming to connect with potential buyers and drive them towards purchasing (or leasing) property.

- **Pharmaceuticals industry**, he would be aiming to connect with doctors and medical professionals and drive them towards using particular brand medical supplies, or getting them to prescribe them to the patients they are treating.

- **Employment services industry**, he would be aiming to connect with employers and drive them towards hiring clients from our caseload.

Can you see how each time our salesperson aims to connect with a particular target-market and the end result is some type of successful sale? This would be true for all salespeople, not just our jobseeker. So that is something you can use to help you work out what the core purpose is for your industry – what is true for all people who hold that particular job title?

Relevant skills matching the role

Now, it is important to note that goals belong to an individual and therefore must genuinely reflect what that jobseeker wants to achieve if they are successful in gaining the job.

Just because we know the core purpose of the role, doesn't mean we should just write a statement to trick hiring managers into considering us – we have to genuinely want to do the job well, and achieve personal satisfaction in some area of the job. Sure it is possible to write a non-genuine statement, but sooner or later the hiring manager is going to work out that you don't have passion for the type of work you do if you don't have passion, which will just ruin the good impression you have worked hard to build into your application.

So, maybe our salesperson just wants to beat the monthly targets he is given by helping to increase revenue and customer relationships so the business grows but he don't aspire to be the absolute best salesperson in the field; whereas a rival salesperson might aim to become the company's Number 1 salesperson, and therefore would want to highlight their strong competitive spirit.

Which salesperson would impress an employer the most would fully depend on what the employer is wanting, needing and expecting from potential employees. Maybe they just want some who is solid and consistent, so our salesperson would be more ideal, and the rival would come across as too aggressive. So this is where it becomes helpful to understand not just the industry, and the job role, but also the particular employer.

Let's turn to our salesperson – who is talented and gets results too, after all – let's turn his personal goal of aspiring to increase revenue and customer base so that the business grows into a goal statement, using the formula.

Remember, we started with:

- **My goal is to use my** – fill in the blank with a skill, experience, knowledge, talent, competency, personal attribute etc.

Let's say our salesperson has a natural aptitude for converting leads into purchase transactions, as implied by his dynamic person statement earlier.

So the start of his goal statement would be:

My goal is to use my aptitude for converting leads into purchase transactions...

The next part of the formula was:

- **To** – fill in the blank, answering to do what.

We already know this: our salesperson wants to increase revenue and customer relations...

So our sentence, so far, now reads:

My goal is to use my aptitude for converting leads into purchase transactions to increase revenue and customer relations...

And now all we need to do is round off our sentence.

The last part of the formula was:

- **So that** – fill in the blank with the details showing that he aims to achieve what benefit?

We already know this too: our salesperson wants the business to experience growth as a direct result of his negotiations.

So, our sentence is rounded off to read as:

My goal is to use my aptitude for converting leads into purchase transactions to increase revenue and customer relations so that the business experiences growth as a direct result of my negotiations.

At first glance, that sentence doesn't look like our salesperson has used a formula, but can you see that the sentence has three parts: an introduction, middle and end.

Introductions kick off the sentence, and need to start strong to get readers to read the sentence. Middles must state what you are offering, which is of interest and appeal to the reader, or they'll stop reading; and the end clarifies or states the benefits, or, what is in it for them.

WORKBOOK ACTIVITY TIME!

Okay, we are almost ready for you to head back over to your Student Workbook again, so you can complete the next activity.

In a minute or so, I want you to practice writing Goal Statements. But first, a few instructions.

Firstly, don't just do the activity once; have a few attempts at writing goal statements. Each time, try varying the goal in some way. Come at it from different angles; change up the 'to do what' or 'so you achieve what benefit'

I've given you space to write down three different goal statements. But I'd love it if you do more. So feel free to grab a blank sheet of paper or to print out additional copies of that workbook page so that you can practice, practice, practice.

Once you have completed writing at least three different goal statements, but before you return to the lessons, I want you to read back over each of the statements you end up writing and then firstly, put into words which one is your favourite, and secondly, which is your least favourite, and make sure that for both, you give your reasons why you feel the way you do. Because it really enhances our understanding when we can identify why something works or doesn't work for us enough to put it into words.

I'll end this tutorial now, so that it doesn't get too long and you don't have to keep stopping and re-starting it. When you're finished doing the workbook activities, meet me in the next tutorial.

See you in a short while – but again, take your time and don't rush!

WB03. WRITE GOAL STATEMENTS
Fill in the blanks

Watch Video Tutorial: Write Goal Statements, and then complete the following activities.

3.1	My goal is to use my what? (skills, experience, knowleddge, talent, competency, personal attribute etc)	
	... to (do what?)	
	... so that (you achieve what benefit?)	

Write another one (make it different from the one above)

3.2	My goal is to use my (skills, experience, knowleddge, talent, competency, personal attribute etc)	
	... to (do what?)	
	... so that (you achieve what benefit?)	

Write another one (make it different from both previous attempts)

3.3	My goal is to use my (skills, experience, knowleddge, talent, competency, personal attribute etc)	
	... to (do what?)	
	... so that (you achieve what benefit?)	

Answer Question

3.4	Which of the goal statements do you like best?	☐ 3.1 ☐ 3.2 ☐ 3.3
	Why?	

TUTORIAL 04. CAREER OBJECTIVE Section

This is video 4 of 5 for Lesson: Career Objective section.

Welcome back. I'm so pleased you're back with me again. This is Lesson 03 Tutorial 04 in the Write Your Resume Content module, where we are covering the Career Objective section.

In the last tutorial, I sent you off to complete the workbook activity for writing goal statements.

How did you go with completing the activity?

Most jobseekers tell me that it was way easier than they thought it would be, because of the formula, compared to when they first started this lesson and realised that they were going to have to write one. Formulas are great at making our lives a bit easier aren't they? That's why I spent so much time analysing the resumes to look for common threads.

But, if you did struggle, don't get hung up about it, okay. Maybe writing dynamic person statements are more your thing.

Now, before we move on to writing dynamic person statements, I'd just like to add that it is okay to make minor changes to the actual formula, too; so that you can personalise your statements and not have them look like y   ou have followed a formula.

In Maths, you generally need to follow a formula exactly in order to reach the right answer, but in English, formulas usually just make for good starting, or bouncing off, points.

So, now that you have a sentence that uses the basic formula, you could now take it a next step further by varying your sentence in small ways. For example, instead of starting the sentence with 'my goal is ...' you could play around with alternative ways to kick the sentence off.

Maybe you like the phrase 'I aspire to...' and instead of writing '...to use my...' you might vary it up by writing 'I aspire to [and here you would insert an action]...' For example 'I aspire to sing...', 'I aspire to sell...' 'I aspire to drive...'

That sort of thing.

A word of caution though if you choose to do this: make sure you don't ruin the integrity of the formula. Your aim would be to spruce the sentence up so it doesn't look like you have used a formula, not deviate too far off the formula's path that you don't end up back in typical career objective territory.

If you want to go and do that, then you can pause or stop the video now and come back when you are done. Otherwise, we'll crack on now to learn how to write dynamic person statements.

Dynamic Person Statements

Whereas the key to writing a good goal statement is to understand the core purpose of a job role, the key to writing a good dynamic person statement is to know your own particular strengths and personal attributes that match the needs of the job role, so you can then laden the sentence with strong words that demonstrate how great you are. (It is an opportunity for you to sell your key skills and achievements, and to brag about your higher value! So embrace this chance to talk positive about yourself.)

We can partly formula-ise a dynamic person statement too, as guidance to help us create a unique and powerfully written statement. But the formula is not quite as clear-cut as it was for the goal statement.

So, what's the formula I came up with:

- **A** - then fill in the blank that follows with a strong adjective
- Fill in the second blank again, this time fill it with a position title or other relevant title or label,
- **With** – fill in the third blank with a bold claim following the connecting word 'with'
- **In** – fill in the last blank with supportive details that demonstrate benefits and value related to that bold claim following the connecting word 'in'.

> **A** _____ [strong adjective] _____ [position title or other relevant label] **with** _____ [a bold claim] **in** _____[supporting details that demonstrate benefits and value].

But remember that a sentence in the career objection position of the resume must be written using third-person viewpoint, to replicate that the words are being spoken by (unidentified) someone else about the candidate (which is our own self).

You should notice that our dynamic person statement also follows the basic structure of writing quality three part sentences because it too uses: an introductory opener; has a 'middle' and then a conclusion-based ending.

You'll remember that introductions kick off a sentence and need to start strong in order to get the reader reading, and that the middle must state what you are offering which is of interest and appeal to the reader – which your bold claim should be aiming for anyway, and then end clarifies or states the benefits, or 'what's in it for them' so they can see the value.

Let's return to our salesperson and revisit what he wrote in our earlier tutorial, and then we'll break down how he has met each part of the formula.

A talented Salesperson with proven history in following up leads and referrals, and converting discussion into opportunities and sale transactions.

The **first blank** – a strong adjective

As you can see, our salesperson has chosen the word 'talented' as his strong adjective. So his sentence opens as:

> *A talented...*

You don't have to start your dynamic person statements with the words 'A talented...' You might like to open your sentence with other descriptors, such as, 'A personable...', 'a friendly...', 'a capable...'

Choose a key personal attribute or strength that you possess and are comfortable in expressing.

The **second blank** – a position title or other relevant title or label

Adjectives describe or qualify the nouns and pronouns that come after them, so this leads us immediately to our second blank.

Our second blank needs to specify what he has just described as talented. This word could be a formal position title, an informal position title or another relevant label that the person gives themself. Because the purpose of the sentence is job related, it makes sense for candidates to label what they do for a living or as their career.

So, our salesperson can title or label himself as a salesperson to round off the sentence opening and make the introductory element complete. So his dynamic person statement so far reads as:

> *A talented Salesperson...*

Now that we have the introductory opener completed, it enables us to get straight into the heart of what we really want our reader to know about who we are and what we do.

The word 'with' is used to connect the first part of the sentence with the next part – the middle, which will be our third fill in the blank.

The **third fill in the blank** – a bold claim.

Our sales person's bold claim that he wants his readers to know about himself as a candidate is that he has 'proven history' in the details that follow. So his statement now reads as:

A talented Salesperson with proven history...

Now our salesperson has a history in sales and in following up on leads and referrals, and turning everyday general conversations with strangers into opportunities to do business for his employer, and has a fantastic and strong track record of leading those people into purchasing his company's products or services. He has previous managers who sing his praises over his natural talent to do this, so he should have no qualms about using the phrase in his sentence.

But, it is important to note here: you should only provide a bold claim that your referees will fully, immediately and unreservedly back you up on, or your great start to your resume will soon take an unfortunate nose-dive back to the 'not-for-us' pile when the employer reaches their round of fact checking, that we were fully aiming to avoid.

In many ways, a dynamic person statement is mostly for those that are top performers in something, like our high performing salesperson; as a way for them to say 'you've received an application from the best of the best', and so it is more common to see a dynamic person statement in a Combination resume rather than a Functional resume.

But, just because they aren't used to seeing dynamic person statements in functional resumes (because of the jobseeker groups that generally need to use this format), doesn't mean we can't teach hiring managers to start seeing and expecting them.

So, please feel free to include one, if you want.

But, if you do, never use words like 'proven history' if you cannot prove it within your history or if you are only building up your skill or experience levels.

Instead, you could boldly claim something like 'a passion for...', 'an interest in...' or some other such honestly-worded phrase, so that it transitions your readers from your opening over to your supportive details.

Remember, there is never a good reason to be dishonest in your application; and the consequences can have a seriously negative impact on your employability – and not now and just in the short term but it could come back to bite you on the butt over a much longer period too.

Okay, are you ready to head back over to complete the next lot of Student Workbook activities?

Before I send you to do this, I want you to keep two things in mind:

Firstly, many people have trouble saying nice things about themselves, let alone writing something strong and positive. If you struggle at all with the following activity, then perhaps start by writing about someone else – we don't give out enough compliments to others, so train yourself to start doing so by finding nice things to say about nice and not so nice people; and then when you are ready, write down how wonderful you are, as though you are another person who absolutely needs to rave how fantastic you are.

And secondly, while you are completing the activity, remember to keep the job you seek to gain in mind, so you can match the nice things you will say about yourself so that it is also interesting and appealing to your potential employers. Again, I've provided space for you to write three dynamic person statements but feel free to practice more on blank paper or on additional pages of the workbook.

I'll see you back in the next tutorial once you've finished. Remember, don't rush through completing your activities, take your time and find lots of nice things to say!

WB04. WRITE DYNAMIC PERSON STATEMENT

Answer Questions:

4.1	What aspect of the job role are you particularly good at?	
4.2	Does this align strongly with what the employer's key focus is?	☐ Yes ☐ No
	Why / why not?	

Fill in the Blanks
Write a Dynamic Person statement

4.3	[insert strong adjective]	A...
	[insert position title or other relevant label	

	[insert a bold claim]	... with ...
	[insert supporting details that demonstrates benefits and value]	... in ...

Write another Dynamic Person statement (make your bold claim and supporting details different to your first statement

4.4	[insert strong adjective]	A...
	[insert position title or other relevant label	
	[insert a bold claim]	... with ...

	[insert supporting details that demonstrates benefits and value]	... in ...

Write a Dynamic Person statement (make your strong adjective and label different from your first and second statement; and make your bold claim and supporting details different from both statements already written)

4.5	[insert strong adjective]	A...
	[insert position title or other relevant label	
	[insert a bold claim]	... with ...
	[insert supporting details that demonstrates benefits and value]	... in ...

Write a Dynamic Person statement (make the entire dynamic person statement different from each of the above again)

4.6		A...
	[insert strong adjective]	
	[insert position title or other relevant label	
	[insert a bold claim]	... with ...
	[insert supporting details that demonstrates benefits and value]	... in ...

Answer Question

4.7	Which of the Dynamic Person statements do you like best?	☐ 4.4 ☐ 4.5 ☐ 4.6
	Why?	

TUTORIAL 05. CAREER OBJECTIVE Section

This is video 5 of 5 for Lesson: Career Objective section.

Welcome back. This is Lesson 03 Tutorial 05 in the Write Your Resume Content module. We are still covering the Career Objective section.

How did you go with writing dynamic person statements? Hopefully you found plenty of nice things to say about yourself and are feeling good for having done so.

So now that you've learned how to write both goal statements and dynamic person statements, I have 1 or a couple of questions that you need to answer:

Question 1. Do you want to include a – and I'm using air quotes here again – 'career objective' section in your resume?

If you answered no, you don't want to include this section in your resume; that is perfectly okay. You can simply now mark this lesson as complete and head straight on over to the next lesson because the rest of this video is irrelevant for you.

If you answered yes, you do want to include the section in your resume, knowing that you should write either a goal statement or a dynamic person statement rather than a typical career objective, I have two more questions for you.

The first is:

> *Which type of statement did you prefer? Goal or Dynamic Person?*

And, the second is:

> *Are you happy with any particular goal or dynamic person statement that you wrote while completing your workbook activities?*

If the answer is no, then it would be best if you go back and write a goal or dynamic person statement with the aim of including it in your functional resume.

If you answered yes, then you've already done the hard work – and well done! You can now add your best statement to the Functional Format Resume Worksheet found at the rear of the Student Workbook. And once you've done that, then you too can mark this lesson as completed and then head over to the next lesson.

As always, thank you for watching. I hope you are enjoying the course and finding that resume writing isn't quite as bad as you imagined or first believed it to be before you commenced this course. See you in the next lesson!

WB05. CHOOSE STATEMENT FOR YOUR RESUME

Review the Goal and Dynamic Person Statement activities and compare what you chose as your best goal statement (activity 3.4) against the one you chose as your best dynamic person statement (activity 4.7).

Answer Questions:

5.2	Which do you like best from the two? The Goal Statement or Dynamic Person Statement?	☐ Goal Statement ☐ Dynamic Person Statement
	Why?	
5.3	Do you want to include a 'Career Obective' section in your resume?	☐ Yes - Please now complete 5.4 ☐ No - You can skip 5.4 and move on to the next lesson
5.4		Re-write your preferred statement in the space provided in the Functional Resume Master Worksheet at the back of the Student Workbook.

LESSON 04.

CORE SKILLS SECTION

LESSON INTRO

Welcome to Lesson 04 Core Skills in the Develop Your Resume Content module.

The Core Skills section is the second Summary Information component that we include in our Functional resume.

In this lesson's video tutorials, we will look at five key areas related to Core Skills:

These are:

1. What a Core Skills section is
2. What a typical Core Skills section looks like
3. What alternatives – if any – you can use
4. How to decide on details to include in your Core Skills section, and
5. How to write those details so that they are likely to be interesting to a Hiring Manager.

This lesson is the largest for this entire course because it covers our most essential section of all. So, get your learning caps on and be ready to complete plenty of workbook activities, and I'll see you in the first tutorial.

TUTORIAL 01. CORE SKILLS Section

This is video 1 of 8 for Lesson: Core Skills section.

Thank you for joining me again. I'm really pleased that you are progressing through the course, and hope you are finding the lessons and resources helpful and value-packed.

This video is the first tutorial for Lesson 4 Core Skills in the Develop Your Resume Content module of the Write a Functional Resume course.

In most Functional Resumes, you will find 2 key sections positioned within the Prime Resume Real Estate area (or PRRE).

Those 2 sections are a:

- Personal Profile section, and a
- Core Skills section.

More often than not, the Personal Profile section is listed first, followed by the Core Skills section. But I think this is a big mistake, which I'll give my reasons for in a moment once I've explained what both sections are.

You see, at first glance, the Core Skills section looks quite similar to the Personal Profile section (which should not be confused with the Personal Details section which was our name and contact details).

Because both the Core Skills and Person Profile sections are vitally important in causing a hiring manager to consider you potentially suitable to their vacancy, and these two sections actually work in partnership with each other, I will take you through the Core Skills first but will address the differences or similarities when they arise.

But, before I get into the specifics for the Core Skills section, I'll briefly discuss the power and benefits to these two sections to give you a basic understanding.

The Core Skills and Personal Profile sections together are what make a Functional resume 'functional'.

The word 'functional' means 'having a special activity, purpose, or task.' And, it is the purpose or task of these two sections collectively to show your suitability to the role being sought.

If the details fail to demonstrate suitability to that role, then the resume is simply not fulfilling its purpose.

Now, I don't usually like to talk about the other resume formats in this course, because it can make things confusing, but as I think what I'm about to say will actually increase your understanding, so I'll make an exception.

In chronological and combination format resumes, it is the person's detailed work history listings that serve the purpose of needing to show suitability to the role sought, because that is where all the finer details are fleshed out in those resume formats.

But, because we have chosen the Functional resume format, where our work history (if we even have any) is simple and very low on the details; and the duties and responsibilities we have gained from previous roles and situations have been separated or divorced away from the source from whence it was gained, we need to flesh out our key employability skills within these two sections.

Both the Core Skills section and the Personal Profile section at their most basic are simply bullet lists of what need to be interesting and relevant-to-the-position details about ourselves.

The Core Skills section will be all about the job role (being applied to) and how the particular skills (and experiences) you possess mean you will be able to do the job and do it well, which therefore makes you a great candidate for the role.

The Personal Profile section will be all about you and how your particular personality, interests and talents further aligns you to the role.

Now, an advantage that you gain over jobseekers who choose the Chronological resume format is that you gain 2 areas to demonstrate your key strengths over their one work history listing – and, your listings appear sooner within the document too, which gives you a second slight edge! So we need to make best use of that edge while we can.

Why listing Personal Profile section first is a mistake.

I mentioned a moment ago, many jobseekers, templates that you find online or in resume books, and even most resume writer's, position the Personal Profile section before the Core Skills section, and I believe this is a big mistake.

My reason for this is:

Before any hiring manager wants to learn about any particular candidates personal attributes, they are specifically interested in learning if the candidate has the particular skills and experiences they are looking for – and that information is what they will find in our Core Skills section, isn't it?

If they are interested in what you are like as a person once they have satisfied themself that you have the basics of what they want, need and expect, then they will go looking for what personal attributes you have.

So, how I see it is that to put the Personal Profile section first is like proverbially putting the cart in front of the horse. Sure, the horse might still be able to move the carriage this way if you adjust the riggings a little bit but the actual task will be harder for the poor horse – as well as dangerous with them not being able to see where they are going.

And that is how I see putting the Personal Profile section before the Core Skills is like.

Remember, our job is to make reviewing our application as easy as we can make it for the hiring manager. Remember too, that when an English person reads or skim reads a resume we do so in a left to right downward sweeping motion. So reading becomes harder if we start having to jump back and forth around a document in order to answer the questions as we ask them.

In the last lesson I described to you a Hiring Manager's reading behaviour when they first approach reviewing applications. If we go back to that, we can see that so far our hiring manager has mentally checked off that our Personal Details are present and accounted for, and that some will and the rest won't have read our Career Objective statement (if we included one).

Which means that for half our hiring manager's performing their initial skim read review they still know absolutely nothing about us yet – and therefore are still seeking to answer their initial hiring questions – which we already appreciate that we need to start answering immediately.

The other half of our hiring managers, the ones who did read and were impressed by our Career Objective statement have now moved on to their secondary rounds of hiring questions, so are probably on the lookout right now for specific details related to what we mentioned in our statement.

The logical place for them to find those specifics in a Chronological or Combination format resume is in the applicants Work History section.

But as we've already covered, the Functional format uses the Core Skills and Personal Profile sections to provide the substance that hiring managers need to help make their decision, not our low-detailed work history section. And, because we want the hiring manager to keep finding details that are interesting and relevant to their needs and wants, it is only logical that we make it as easy for them to locate those specific details as we possibly can, without any great effort or delay in finding them!

So, that is the importance of the 2 sections in conjunction with each other and why I believe we should include the Core Skills section before the Personal Profile section. Now let's look at the Core Skills section on its own.

What is a Core Skills section

The Core Skills section is simply a bullet listing.

The function this section serves is to demonstrate how the particular job-specific and job-relevant skills and experiences that you possess match the needs and requirements of job role so that it demonstrates not only that you can do that particular type of job, but could do it well.

Where many jobseekers go wrong is they treat the resume as a list of everything about themself, which creates a vague picture of who they are as a potential employee. What we are aiming to achieve is include specific details about our self that paints a vivid mental picture of us being capable for our chosen job type, so the information is tailored to the specific job role.

Once again, we should look at things from the hiring perspective.

If I was reviewing applications for, say, a Forklift Driver position, I would have a couple of initial hiring questions that I would need answering floating around in my head:

- Does this person have Forklift Driving experience?
- Do they have a Forklift Driver's Licence?
- Is that licence current?

And:

- How much Forklift Driving experience do they have?
- What sort of goods did they load and unload?
- What volume of good did they move?

Those sorts of questions.

My priority as hiring manager would be to gain answers to those specific questions – especially the first one 'Does this person have Forklift Driving experience?'

Once I gained answers to those types of job-related initial questions, I'd then formulate secondary hiring questions, which is likely to be more focused on the person, like:

- Were they any good?
- Were they reliable?
- What was their behaviour like?
- Are there any problems I need to

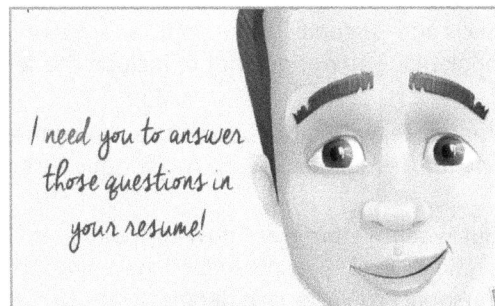

I need you to answer those questions in your resume!

be wary of?

So our Core Skills section must house the answers to the job-role related questions (and our Personal Profile should try to answer as many typical to the role secondary hiring questions that a hiring manager might ask themself too).

Now, it is important to note here that some recruiters do hire people without previous experience, and getting through to being considered comes down to how impressed the hiring managers are by your resume. If you paint a strong enough mental picture of capability, you'll get the break that you are hoping for because your application will beat every applicant who has sent in a terrible job application.

I, like many hiring managers, would much rather hire someone who has the necessary education and licensing etc but does not have firsthand experience in the role than to hire a person who has years of experience but doesn't instil me with any confidence that they will do the job well and non-problematically.

What does a typical Core Skills section look like?

The key aspect of the Core Skills section, as mentioned earlier, is that the information is presented in bullet list form.

There are a number of different ways that we can present this section on paper, which we will address in the module Create and Stylise your Functional Resume Document – for those of you who are enrolled in the premium version of this course.

The important part as we develop our content is just that we will be creating a bullet list of job-relevant information.

What alternatives – if any – you can use

Again, as I mentioned earlier: your functional resume would simply not be a functional resume if you do not include the Core Skills and Personal Profile sections.

You choose to either include these sections in your functional resume or you leave one or both out – but, of course, now that you know how vitally important both the Core Skills and Personal Profile sections are to a functional resume; you would be completely bonkers if you decided not to include the sections.

Therefore, within the big picture view context, there are no alternatives that we could use for this section like we had for our Career Objective section.

But when we progress now to looking at the 'what information to include within this section' level, you do indeed have two choices when creating your Core Skills and Personal Profile section details.

Those choices are to write in either:

1. Sentence form, or
2. Word (or short phrase) list form

So let's briefly discuss these choices.

Sentence form

Sentence form means writing out a complete skill or personal attribute statement so that the sentence contains specifics and quantifiable results to substantiate the skill or attribute under discussion. I clarified what skill and personal attribute statements are back in Lesson 02.

But remember, skill statements looked similar to this:

- Answer 100 telephone calls per day using PABX system (answering phones)
- Provide relevant product information to facilitates customers purchasing of Manchester-department products (product knowledge or sales skills)

And personal attribute statements looked like this:

- Arrive on time to open branch for staff to set up and prepare for day's trading.
- Pitch in to serve customers during high volume periods

As you may have already guessed, we write skill statements in our Core Skills section, and personal attribute statements in our Personal Profile section.

Our other choice was word (or short phrase) list form.

Word (or short phrase) list form

Word or Phrase list form means listing the details by either specifying the skill by name (which is micro level) or by implying a range of skills through listing the skill category (which is macro level).

For example

- Customer Service (micro)
- Typing (micro)
- Driving (micro)
- Computer skills (macro)

That's the 2 options available to you.

But here's the secret to standing out and impressing the hiring manager: *Functional resumes need to use sentence form, not word or short phrase list form.*

This means that not only will you need to cover the scope of what skills and experiences are needed in the job role, but you will also need to write strong skill statements in your Core Skills section for them.

Not doing this is the main cause of most jobseekers going wrong with creating their own resume unassisted, which ultimately causes their applications to rejected by the majority of recruiters. Because the specifics that hiring managers want to read are missing; which means they don't make a mental picture of the person doing the work as they review the resume; which means, they can't see the capability or suitability of the applicant and therefore conclude the applicant is unsuitable to their needs and wants.

Back when you went to Primary School, did your teacher ever get you to do Show and Tell? Where you brought in an item from home to show classmates and had to tell them a little bit about it?

Well, resume writing uses the Show and Tell concept as well.

If we look back at our Career Objective statements, we entice the reader about what they can expect by telling them a little bit about our self as we filled in the blanks with words or short phrases; but within our Core Skills and Personal Profiles sections we must show them our capabilities in relation to each skill.

Let me restate to you what I said earlier about what the Core Skills section is:

The function this section serves is to demonstrate how the particular job-specific and job-relevant skills and experiences that you possess match the needs and requirements of job role so that it demonstrates not only that you can do that particular type of job, but could do it well.

The word 'demonstrate' is a synonym of the word 'show'. The two words mean the same thing. A simple way to distinguish the difference between showing and telling in resume writing is this:

Sentence form = Show
Word or short phrase lists = Tell

In the next tutorial, we will start looking at how to decide what details to include in our Core Skills section, and then progress to learning how to write out those skill statements so that the details are effective in maintaining a good impression so that the hiring manager becomes or remains interested in you as a potentially suitable candidate.So, I'll

meet you over in the next tutorial.

TUTORIAL 02. CORE SKILLS Section

This is video 2 of 8 for Lesson: Core Skills section.

Welcome back. You are still in Lesson 04 Core Skills section in the Develop Your Resume Content module for the Write A Functional Resume course. This is the second tutorial for this lesson.

In the last tutorial, we discussed that a Core Skills section is a must-have when creating a Functional resume and that the purpose of this section is to include details of the skills and experiences you have that would make you suitable to the type of job you are seeking to gain, and that you will need to Show those details, not Tell.

In this short tutorial, we will cover firstly how to decide which skills and experiences you should include in this section, and in future tutorials we will then look at how we can write those details so that the specifics are interesting to the hiring manager.

There will be a number of Workbook Activities for you to complete at the end of this lesson.

So let's get straight into it, shall we.

How to decide on details to include in your Core Skills section

It is rare for any job to only have one task involved.

Usually, each position has a couple of different tasks that the position holder will need to do as an ordinary part of their duties. Naturally, some jobs will have a wide variety of tasks; others will be narrower; it all depends on the type of work you seek because it will be different to every position, industry and employer.

The main thing here is that we need to cover each of the core tasks common to most vacancies within this section if we want to fully demonstrate to the hiring manager that we are potentially the right person for them.

For example, a forklift driver might only have a few tasks to complete, such as:

- Operate the forklift to move goods from one place to another, such as on and off trucks, but they might also
- Fill in paperwork
- Need to perform some manual labour
- Keep the forklift fuelled up and in good working order

Whereas, a real estate salesperson would have a wider range of tasks to complete, such as:

- Making phone calls,
- Completing paperwork
- Driving to locations
- Performing property value research
- Meeting and greeting clients to drum up new listings
- Meeting and greeting potential buyers or renters to encourage a sale or lease on their listed property
- Provide advice to landlords and vendors
- Drawing up contracts
- Filing

And much, much more.

Therefore, it is imperative that you have one specific job role in mind when creating a functional resume.

I know, I know, some of you are happy to accept different types of work, and I'm not saying you shouldn't do that. What I am saying is: if you want to apply for different types of jobs, then you will need to pick the main job role that you want to gain and create your resume for that one particular job type. You can then go back and create core skills section for each other type of work you want to gain later, and build a separate resume for each job role so that your applications are always targeted and tailored.

ACTIVITY TIME!

In a moment, I'm going to end this tutorial so that I can send you off to go and complete a Student Activity.

Only this time, you won't be heading to your Student Workbook just yet, and you won't just be completing the activity to help you write the content for your Core Skills section; the activity I'm going to get you to do will be used to help us also develop the content in other lessons for this course too – like writing the content for your Personal Profile, Education and Work History sections as well.

Therefore, it is important that you complete this side-activity. So first, the instructions.

I want you to head online and find 3 to 5 job advertisements for the job role that you are seeking to gain. For example, if you are aiming to get a forklift driver position, then you will need to find 3 to 5 job advertisements for forklift driving roles, whereas if you are aiming to gain a position as a real estate property manager, then you would need to find 3 to 5 job advertisements for property managing roles.

Now, it is okay if those 3 to 5 job advertisements are not vacancies that you will ever apply to – perhaps you find a job advertisement for a vacancy in a different state or territory. The goal here is to go to a popular job board for your country, find – and print out – 3 to 5 job advertisements that best represent the type of work you are seeking to gain.

3 job advertisements is the minimum you should find; 5 or more would be more ideal.

What we are going to do in this exercise is maximise our chance of appealing to the widest number of employers as we can by examining each of those job advertisements and marking up specific things with a view of finding common threads, so that we learn with greater clarity what the hiring managers and recruiters are looking for, for the type of job you want – because, those job advertisement will teach us what things they mentally want to tick off when they review applications. Of course, not all job adverts will cover everything about a role, so although we will find some skills and duties etc repeated across each of the job ads; it's the other aspects that we are looking to learn here too.

When I've done this exercise in group training sessions, I have found that the best and easiest way to get participants seeing and understanding what I want them to see and understand is through getting them to print out their advertisements and mark up with a variety of coloured highlighter pens.

So, we'll need 7 different colours for this activity.

Now, if you don't have seven different colours or you aren't able to print the job ads out, that's okay. I still want you to complete this activity, so you will just need to adapt the instructions I give you in whatever way you can so that you can identify the seven different areas that I want you to be able to see visually.

For example, you might be able to electronically highlight the advertisements instead of printing the ads out; or, if say you only have 3 different coloured highlighters, then you might circle the text to represent one colour but underline text with the same colour to represent using two different colours, and then just use a pencil or pen as the seventh colour – that sort of thing.

I'll leave the specifics of how you go about it, up to you.

So, I'll end this tutorial here so that you can go and find your 3 to 5 job advertisements. When you are done, meet me in the next tutorial with your advertisements and pens handy.

Okay, see you there in a short while.

TUTORIAL 03. CORE SKILLS Section

This is video 3 of 8 for Lesson: Core Skills section.

Welcome back. You are still in Lesson 04 Core Skills section in the Develop Your Resume Content module for the Write A Functional Resume course. This is the third tutorial for this lesson.

At the end of the last tutorial, I sent you off to find 3 to 5 job advertisements that best represent the type of work you want to gain.

In this short tutorial, I will provide you with instructions on how I want you to mark up those job advertisements, as the information will help us complete the rest of Lesson 04 Core Skills section, as well as activities in the Personal Profile and other lessons found later on in this course.

So, let's get started on the Mark-Up Activity.

We are going to colour-code our job advertisements so that when we are finished we can assess 7 different areas to help us with writing our resume content so that we gives ourselves the best opportunity to address what employers of that particular job role want, need and expect when they review applications.

This is where our 7 different highlighter pens come in. We are going to use one colour for each of the 7 different areas we will later analyse.

Now, I don't care which colour(s) you use for which aspect, we are just aiming to colour-code our job advertisements.

Personally, I think it is easiest if you work with one colour and mark up each of your different job advertisements with that one colour before moving on to the next colour. But if you want to work differently, that is okay. As long as we end up with the same colour coded system in the end.

This is how I want you to mark up your job advertisements. Use:

Colour One –to mark all Skills that you find mentioned in the ad. Remember, skills are what we can do.

Then, use:

Colour Two –to mark all Duties or Responsibilities that you see mentioned in the ad. These are the tasks and responsibilities that you would hold in the job.

Colour Three – to mark all Personal Attributes that you see mentioned in the ad. Remember, personal attributes are our characteristics or personal traits, or what we are like as a person.

Colour Four – to mark any volume amounts specified.

Colour Five – to mark any results and outcomes that employers have mentioned they are expecting within the ad.

Colour Six – to mark all Training, Education, Qualifications and or Licensing that you see mentioned – both essential and desirable.

Colour Seven – to mark any other expectations or requirements mentioned but not falling into one of the other six colour categories.

Now it is important to note here, that not all job advertisements will have all of the seven components that I'm getting you to identify; so don't worry if you find you only need to use less highlighters.

And, if you have any difficulty with completing this activity, please take a look at the Sample Mark Up that I have provided for you in the resource section and use it as a guide.

Okay, I'm going to end this tutorial here, so that you can spend as much time as you need carefully completing this activity. When you are finished, meet me in the next tutorial where we will start extracting the information we want and need for our Core Skills section.

See you in the next tutorial.

TUTORIAL 04. CORE SKILLS Section

This is video 4 of 8 for Lesson: Core Skills section.

Welcome back. You are still in Lesson 04 Core Skills section in the Develop Your Resume Content module for the Write a Functional Resume course. This is the fourth tutorial for this lesson.

At the end of the last tutorial, I sent you off to go and mark up the 3 to 5 job advertisements that best represent the type of work you want to gain, so that we can easily see 7 different aspects about those job advertisements.

Hopefully, your printouts should now have splashes of different colour.

Obviously, any text you needed to mark with colours one and two, are best suited to be addressed in your Core Skills section – because the spotlight for these aspects is clearly on the job role.

Any text that was marked using colour three is more suitable to be addressed in your Personal Profile section – because personal attributes are focused entirely on you as a person.

Any text that we marked with colours four and five we will examine in both the Core Skills and the Personal Profile section lessons, as these golden nuggets provide us with great insight into how hiring managers might view our potential fit – The amount levels or results from our previous roles and situations will enable us to see if our levels are in line with what employers are looking for, which will help us make decisions on how we might handle things if we happen to be over or under those specifics volume levels, so we can work out whether the difference may be problematic for our applications or candidacy.

If you have any text that has been marked using colour six, these may be things we need to address in our Historical Information sections – if we hold the appropriate qualification, license or permit etc and or have completed training; so we will deal with these in Lesson 06 of the Develop Your Resume Content module.

And, finally, any text that we marked with colour seven, is an employer consideration that we need to try to factor somewhere in our application so that we are adequately covering the full range of what we now know the employers are looking for. So we will need to work out whether the best place to address that in our resume, our cover letter, in an application form (if employer requires one), in other supportive application documents like Statements Addressing Selection Criteria, or even in person during a job interview.

Now, if you were to lay out each of the job advertisements next to each other, you are likely to see that each advertisements is marked up with at least the first four colours. And, if you look at each advertisement in turn, you will probably see for colour one, the main skills needed in the job role are highlighted in each of the advertisements. This is to be expected.

You may notice that some employers provided more information about their vacancy than other job advertisements. For example, that some employers may require their employees to do a wider range of tasks within the role compared to other employers. And that is to be expected too.

Another thing you might notice is that some employers don't mention the core skill requirements for the role at all, because they address the other things that are important to them and treat the basic essentials as 'a given' that they don't need to go into too much detail over. This is to be expected too.

Just remember though, that just because one employer doesn't list a particular skill doesn't mean they don't want, need or expect it – they may have listed it as a Duty instead, or limited their ad description so that it keeps the cost down or something.

But, because we've used so many different colours, and many of the details are repeated, it can make it quite confusing to narrow down on what the employers are looking for properly during the next step when we develop our core skills content.

So, before we get to working on our Core Skills section, I will get you to do one more side-activity, where we will manipulate our highlights and enter them into our Student Workbook so that it will make it easier for us later.

The activities we will complete are WB06 through to WB12.

What I want you to do is:

First, looking only at what you used as colour one, as you complete the activity, I want you to 1. Group related skills into categories so they are close together and 2. write each of the skills and categories from each of the ads into the space provided in the Student Workbook, which is WB06. This will enable us to have a clear view of what skills the employer is after.

If you are seeking work as a Forklift Driver for example, you are most likely to find that each job advertisement mentions Forklift Driving somewhere within the ad. This could be either as a skill or as a Duty, or even just as the advertisement title.

Now, we only want to list something once in our workbook, so, in the space provided write this core skill as a skill rather than a duty.

Some categories you might group your skills into could be:

- Core Job Skills / Technical Knowledge
- Administration
- Communication
- Computer
- Business Development
- Self-Management
- Health and Safety
- Financial
- Managerial

And or whatever other categories you come up with and feel the skill best fits as.

Also, if you like staying organised, as you transfer your information across to your workbook you might like to strikethrough your highlights with a pen or pencil after you've dealt with each highlight, or put a little tick somewhere so that you can see that it's been done – but you don't have to do this additional step, if you don't want to.

I just do this – the little tick against a mark up bit – when I write resumes for clients because it helps me to filter out all the extra stuff and allows me to just focus on what aspects I need to ensure I get into my clients resumes; and I like keeping myself organised even though it means a bit of extra handwriting.

The reason I'm getting you to transfer the information from your printouts to your workbook is so that we create a clear simple list of all of the different skills these employers have told us are important to them so we only have to see each point once, and can do so easily. The lists we create will then provide us with a good idea as to the scope of skills and things we need to cover in our resume.

Once you have worked your way into developing a nice list for the skills, I'll get you to go back through and do the same for the other 6 areas that we marked up, transferring the information into the appropriate part of the workbook (which are activities WB07, WB08, WB09, WB10, WB11 and WB12); so we have nice clear lists ready and waiting for us when we get up to future lessons where we will look at those other areas.

Okay, so I will end this tutorial here so that you can go and start transferring the information. Once you are done, meet me in the next tutorial where we will resume working on developing our Core Skills section content.

(OPTIONAL) MARK-UP ACTIVITY
This section is provided to help those students who prefer to remain organised.

WB06 – Identify the Core Skills (Colour One)

(Category)		(Skill)	
Technical Skill		...Drive forklift	
Administration		... Create invoices	

WB 07 – Duties and Responsibilities Identified (Colour Two)

e.g. Report faulty machinery to supervisors

WB08 – Personal Attributes (Colour Three)

e.g. Learn Quickly	

WB09 – Volume Amounts (Colour Four)

e.g. Type 65 wpm	↓		

WB10 - Results and Outcomes (Colour Five)

e.g. Meet KPI of 5 sales p.m.	=		

WB11 - Training, Education, Qualifications and or Licensing (Colour Six)

e.g. Forklift Licence, Certificate III in Warehouse Operations

WB12 – Other Relevant (Colour Seven)

TUTORIAL 05. CORE SKILLS Section

This is video 5 of 8 for Lesson: Core Skills section.

Welcome back. You are still in Lesson 04 Core Skills section in the Develop Your Resume Content module for the Write a Functional Resume course. This is the fifth tutorial for this lesson.

Yay! Thanks for bearing with me getting you to do all that writing.

Okay, so we have marked up job advertisements and now transferred the details we will need into our Workbook so we can see the key requirements easily, I have one last mini side-task for you to complete before we can begin working on developing the content for your Core Skills section.

Our mini-task will be to relook at what we wrote in activity WB07 Duties and Responsibilities:

Do you have any information in there?

You see, usually Duties and Responsibilities involve a skill of some sort, so technically we should try to identify what particular skill is being asked for in each of what you have listed, and if it is not already in our skills list, we should add it so our skill list is more complete and our duty list is reduced.

So shortly, I'll get you to pause this video so you can return to your student workbook, and look more closely at the duties and responsibilities you added earlier.

But I want you to fully understand why I am meaning, and the reason why I'll be getting you to do that. So, I'll use the forklift driving example again to make my point.

Let's say that each of the job advertisements that you marked up specified forklift driving as a duty rather than a skill. Well, really, forklift driving is a skill as well as a workplace duty, isn't it?

Because our Functional resume format deals with skills not duties, we want (and need) to make sure that we capture this highly essential job role skill in our resume – because it is of high importance to employers.

See, if we were to look at this employer consideration as only a Duty, we would

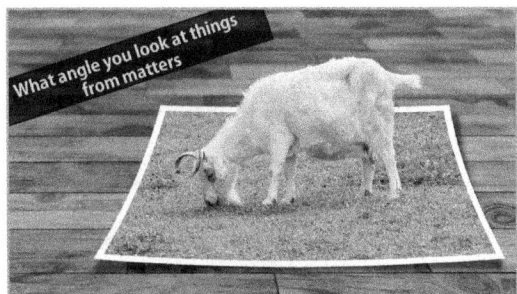

What angle you look at things from matters

probably be tempted to just view this from the angle of *'Have any of my previous roles required me to drive a forklift?'*

Now, if you could answer that question with a yes, then you would willingly accept that you have forklift driving experience, and would have no qualms about adding the detail to your core skills section.

But, for all those who would answer that question with a no, they would be more likely to conclude that they don't have forklift driving experience as a result of the angle that they are coming at – and therefore would feel unable to include this skill in their resume – which means they are going to have a tough-time getting to the job interview stage – unless they lie.

I'm going to get you to make a small mindset shift to encourage you to instead look at forklift driving as a Skill instead of a Duty.

Now, if we were to look at it as a Skill, we would ask the slightly altered question of 'Do I have any experience relating to this skill?' The main emphases there being 'any' instead of 'do I?'

And immediately any person who has undertaken forklift driving training even if they have never held that particular job role previously, would now also be able to honestly answer affirmatively rather than negatively, because as an ordinary part of their course and testing to qualify for a Forklift Licence, they have honestly acquired some experience relating to this skill – even though their experience is limited.

Because, passing the test to be eligible for a licence means that the person has to possess at least a basic level of competency in being able to drive a forklift or they would have failed their testing and therefore don't possess the skill.

For people like me, who have never driven a forklift or undertaken any training on how to drive one, I would have to answer this altered question honestly with a no, just like I would have to do for that first question. But can you see that if you have any experience relating to a particular skill, regardless of where or what circumstance you gained or developed it, means that you now have details to back up you claiming that you posses the skill?

Now, I know, not all of you are going to be applying to forklift driving roles. So, with what you have just learned here in mind, I want you to return to your Student Workbook and relook at your Duties and Responsibilities listing; and, for each and every entry:

1. Identify what skill is involved with the duty or responsibility, and
2. Check if that skill has already been listed or not, and
3. If it is not, add it to your Core Skills list in activity WB06.

You'll notice that in WB07 I have the example text **'*Report faulty machinery to supervisors*'** as a duty I found in an advertisement.

So, what is the skill involved here?

To me, the immediate skill being asked for is to identify when a machine is faulty and then report the matter so that it can be fixed. So the skill is: identify faults.

Reporting to supervisors can also be converted into skills. To report a fault to a supervisor, you would need to either let them know verbally, or in writing. In other words, use written or verbal communication skills.

I hope those two examples give you an idea of how you can turn any of the duties you have listed into skills.

Okay, you go and do this activity, and I'll see you in the next tutorial.

TUTORIAL 06. CORE SKILLS Section

This is video 6 of 8 for Lesson: Core Skills section.

Welcome back. You are still in Lesson 04 Core Skills section in the Develop Your Resume Content module for the Write a Functional Resume course. This is the sixth tutorial for this lesson.

Now we can begin working on developing the content for our Core Skills section.

To create our Core Skills section content, we will need to work incrementally, using the following five steps. We need to work out:

1. If there are any other skills that employers will be looking for that just weren't specified in the job advertisements that we chose to analyse,
2. Which of the skills are the most important or mean the most to the employer, so that we can prioritise the order in which we will present our skills in our Core Skills section,
3. Which of the skills that we know employers are looking for we have some or a lot of personal experience with,
4. Which of the skills we don't have and then make an assessment about how this may affect our application – and work out how we will resolve the issue if not having the skill is likely to be detrimental to our applications, and finally,
5. We then need to convert our list of raw skills into effective and interesting skill statements, so that the hiring manager not only sees that we have the skills they require but also so that they can mentally picture each of our skills in action to maximise our chance of getting them to see our potential suitability and fit.

So we will now start working our way through those 5 steps.

Step One – are all the key skills for the job role listed?

Sorry to do this to you again, but we will need to head over to our student workbook again to be able to complete this easy step.

But don't worry, the activity won't take you very long, so I'll just get you to pause the video and come back when you are finished again like I got you to do in a previous lesson rather than end this tutorial and pick up in another one, or this lesson will end up with a ridiculous number of super short videos.

The first thing we need to do is make sure we have each of the most important skills listed in our workbook.

To complete this step, you will need to think about the specific job role that you seek to gain, and perhaps even do a bit more research if necessary.

You probably have caught the main ones from the job advertisements you found – especially if you grabbed and analysed 5 or more positions, but it is important that we at least explore the idea of making sure we have covered everything important, so that we aren't missing anything super important.

Okay, you can pause the video again so that you review your list of skills in activity WB06 to see if what is required in the job is complete or not.

If feel everything important has been covered, great. If not, you will need to work out what is missing and then add them to your listing.

Have you listed all the main important skills for that type of job?

Step Two – Put the skills into order of priority

Excellent, you should now have a complete list of skills that employers want for the type of work you seek to gain.

Now we are ready for Step Two, which is to look at that list of Skills we have, which is what the employers want, need and expect and now start matching our self to this role.

It is really important that we address an employer's most important and fundamental hiring questions foremost in our resume. So, our next task is to prioritise the list of skills we have in WB06 so that we know which skills we must convert into a skill statements versus what we don't need to worry too much about.

What I want you to do is rank each of your entries, by putting them into number order from most important to least important.

Of course, having experience in the role will help you to determine the order of priority with much more ease than if you don't have experience – so it is important to use your best judgement here if you have not previously worked in this type of role.

If you have any trouble working out what is most important to least important, then it would be a good idea to ask someone you know, 'If you were an employer trying to fill a _____ vacancy – where you fill in the blank with the job role you seek – what skill do you think would be more important?' and see what other people think. The other way is to relook at your marked up job advertisements. Any skill that is listed in each of the advertisements is more likely to be more important that a skill that is only listed in one of the advertisements.

So, you will need to pause this video again, and go and mark your list of skills with a system of your choice that will order the entries. I number mine, starting with one for the most important, with each number after that being the skill is less important.

WB06 – Identify the Core Skills (Colour One)
This space has been included for those of you who would like to rewrite their list into order and so they have a neat master listing.

(Category)		(Skill)	
Technical Skill		...Drive forklift	
Administration		... Create invoices	

Prioritise the skills in WB06 so that it is clear which skills are the most important to least important.

Step Three – Work out which of the skills we have.

So far, our list of Skills has all been about what the employers are looking for in their ideal candidate. Now we need to match the skills we have up to what they want.

In a moment, you will need to pause this video again to return to activity WB06 – Core Skills, to mark each entry listed to indicate if you have the skill and experience or not.

Again, I'll leave it up to you as to how you mark up your workbook, but some suggestions are:

- Place a tick or cross at the beginning or end of the line,
- Write the word Yes or No, or indicate yes or no by writing a Y or N at the beginning or end of the line. Or you could even
- Leave everything that employers are looking for which you can say Yes to, and strike out all skills that you need to say No to.

You'll notice that I have left space for you to be able to put a tick or cross at the beginning or end of the skill.

But. Before you go and do this, I want you to use that slight mindset change that I talked about in the last tutorial.

So again, instead of looking at each skill in your list and asking the typical question, 'Have I done this in a previous job role? I want you to ask the adjusted question for every skill listed:

'Do I have any experience – big or small, gained in or outside of paid employment – relating to this particular skill?'

Step Four – Do you possess all the necessary skills?

Welcome back, again. You are progressing quite nicely!

We are now ready for Step 4, which is working out which of the skills the hiring manager will be looking for, we have too.

Do you have all of the important skills that employers are looking for, for that type of job?

If you do have all the necessary skills and experiences the employers are looking for, then you'll be able to skip ahead to the next tutorial because the rest of this tutorial will not be relevant to you.

But before you leave, I'd like to share one useful tip for gaining jobsearch success with you: as you apply to job vacancies, if you find new skills that seem important, either add them into your resume for that particular vacancy so that you have covered everything that particular employer is looking at, update your resume with that skill so that all future applications are covering that important skills too, as this will maximise your chance of appealing to a wider range of employers.

So, if you are leaving us, you can do so now and head over to the next tutorial.

Now, for those of you who are staying with me.

If you don't have all the necessary skills and experiences, despite looking outside of direct work experience and assessing your transferrable skills, then you will need to spend a bit of time considering how not having all those important skills and experiences could impact upon your job applications, and the actions you might take or measures you could put into place to address your skill gaps which are potential barriers to gaining jobsearch success.

It is outside of the scope of this course to address closing up skill gaps and addressing barriers to employment, but I will briefly mention a couple of things.

Firstly, one of the obvious ways that you could work around skills gaps and barriers would be to apply to entry-level or career starter positions, like apprenticeships, traineeships and junior roles. Each industry and vocation usually has them.

Next, look at ways of building up the required skill level. I don't just mean enrolling in accredited industry or task specific courses here – though that is often a great starting point. I also mean accepting side-positions that will lead to you developing the appropriate skill and experience. These can be alternate positions in the same industry as a paid employee, or it could be doing volunteer work or participating in the community either full time, part time, or casually, or even informal studies or activities done in your own time.

And finally, it is important to note here that not all hiring managers ask the question 'Does the person have experience [gained from a previous role]?'

Many employers just want a person who has the skills they need, and they may be willing to hire you despite you missing one or two skills.

The solution to how to close skill gaps and employment barriers really all depends on the job role you are going for, and each different employer, so addressing the gaps and barriers is an area that you alone will need to consider and address to suit your circumstance.

In the next tutorial, we will move on to our last step in the writing our Core Skills section content, which is using the raw skills list that we now have and converting that list into strong and compelling skill statements so that the details are interesting to hiring managers.

So, I will see you in the next tutorial.

TUTORIAL 07. CORE SKILLS Section

This is video 7 of 8 for Lesson: Core Skills section.

Welcome back. You are still in Lesson 04 Core Skills section in the Develop Your Resume Content module for the Write a Functional Resume course. This is the seventh tutorial for this lesson.

In the previous tutorial, we completed the first four out of five steps to develop a raw list of important job-related and employer-important skills that we can transform into mental picture inducing skill statements that show off our performance competency.

In this tutorial, we will now complete that final fifth step and learn how to transform our sentences.

Step Five – Convert our raw skills list into skill statements

If you look at WB06 a bit closer, you'll notice that the raw list we created uses the Telling style; and as we learned a while back, it is important that we demonstrate our competence to hiring managers.

The best way to do this is by writing custom-written, unique in content evidence and achievement based sentences. In other words, write skill statements that use:

1. Strong, active words
2. Quality descriptions of specific details
3. Numbers and quantities
4. Results and outcomes
5. Past achievements and accomplishments
6. Targeted, positive language

... to briefly and concisely explain the 'who, what, were, when, why and how' particulars, as well as quantifying your results so that it shows the benefits in hiring you.

And, remember how I provided you with a basic formula so that you could write better Goal and Dynamic Person statements? Although I am unable to provide you with a formula that will enable you to write those interesting and compelling skill and personal attribute statements, I can provide you with an equation that we can use to guide us.

We will need to build each skill statement one step at a time, but the basic equation is:

**Strong Active Verb + Specific Supportive Details + Results = Compelling
Skill Statement**

I'll now take you through five steps to buiding skills statements for your resume. Those steps are:

> **Step 1.** Choose a Skill.
> **Step 2.** Choose an appropriate Action Word
> **Step 3.** Add Numbers and Quantifiable Amounts
> **Step 4.** Add Results and Outcomes
> **Step 5.** Ensure targeted, positive language is used

What I will do is guide you through each of the steps from start to finish so that you can get a big picture view and see how I transform skills into skill statements, and then, once you know the basic process, we can then turn to your workbook and get you to start building your own skill statements that you will include in your resume.

So our first step towards writing a skill statement was to:

1. Choose which skill that you are going to transform into a skill statement, and then
2. Select the strongest and most appropriate active verb with which to start your skill statement for that skill off with.

When we have done those two things, we have already successfully completed the first part of the skill statement equation - because Steps 1 and 2 actually go hand in hand with each.

Later, we will be turning each of the skills in our raw list into skill statements, so let's assume we have just picked the first skill listed, our next step is to choose an appropriate action word.

Strong action words

Now, there are so many words in the English language. We often have a choice from different words that all mean the same thing to help us convey our message. Because of this, some words will come across as stronger than others.

When it comes to resume writing, the stronger the words we use are, the better our resume reads, and the more positive and capable we come across.

To iterate this point, notice the difference between the following similar words: 'started' and 'implemented'

We could interpret the word 'started' to mean that a particular task was started, but not necessarily that it was also finished. Whereas we could interpret the word 'implemented' to mean that a system or practice went from not having been done to now being done as standard, or that the system or practice went from not having existed previously and was taken all the way from idea and introduction through to completion.

So, the word 'implemented' in this context conveys a much stronger, more powerful meaning than the word 'started'.

Let's compare another set of similar words: how about 'gained' versus 'won'?

When I see the word 'won', I immediately interpret that considerable personal effort was put into a goal or task, and the desired result's attainment was because of that greater, personal effort. But when I compare it to the word 'gained', I interpret it more as that something fortunate happened, but the same result would have occurred whether the person put in any greater personal effort or not; that it would have happened anyway.

In our resume, we need to use the strongest action words, or Active Verbs, to start our sentences as often as possible, so that each time the word appropriately and adequately conveys the message that we personally took deliberate action to bring about a specific and desired result.

So, for step one in building a skill statement, the skill I'll choose is: 'Managing Staff.'

Now, for step two, I could just choose the word 'Manage' as my sentence starter, because it is a relatively strong, active word, but I personally find that the word 'manage' doesn't quite convey the skill as clearly as I intended compared to the alternative word 'supervise.'

So, the active verb 'Supervise' will be my skill statement starter word.

Now, I know choosing active verbs is a struggle for many jobseekers, and some words are so overused that they have lost their powerfulness with some hiring managers, so in the Resources section, I will give you a link which so that you access viewing a list of over 1200 Action Words to help you kick-start your skill statements, so that you aren't just using the same 20 sentence starters that some jobseekers stick to using – because just choosing different starting words will also set you apart in a positive way.

Okay, so now let's move on to the second part of the skill statement equation, which is actually just an extension of Step 1 – Choose a Skill:

Specific supportive details

Once you have chosen your strong, active verb to start your skill statement, your next task is to provide the specific details that explain the 'who, what, where, when, why and or how' of your skill.

Now, you do not need to explain all of those specifics of a skill (that is, you don't need to cover all of the 'who, what, where, when, why and how'), you just need to explain the most relevant aspects about your chosen skill.

The skill I am explaining relates to managing staff. The word staff becomes the specific supportive detail to our action word.

Now, I could just write:

> *Supervise staff.*

And that would adequately cover the 'who' detail.

But there is a really important question you should always ask when writing skill statements, and that question is: Could I be more specific?

Could I be more specific? Yes, I could.

Let's say I worked in the fast food industry. My staff would be kitchen hand and customer service staff, wouldn't they?

So let's break this down.

Supervised kitchen hand and customer service staff provides more specific supportive details and helps to paint a better mental picture than what 'supervise staff' achieves.

So here's my breakdown.

> **Supervise** (*strong, active verb*) **kitchen hand and customer service** (*specific details*) **staff** (*the 'who'*).

Let's try another skill:

The first step was to choose the skill you are going to transform, wasn't it?

This time I will choose 'selling products' as my skill.

The word 'sell' is a perfectly appropriate and strong action word, so my sentence now reads as: Sell products.

But, the word 'products' is really vague. Everything anybody sells is either a product or service in nature. So, can I be more specific?

Why, yes, I can.

How? By telling you what type of products I sell.

Let's say that I sell pallets of beer cartons because I work as a salesperson for a beer manufacturing company.

Notice I didn't just say, 'Sell beer' or 'Sell beer cartons', I said 'Sell pallets of beer cartons' – because beer and even beer cartons on their own doesn't adequately describe 'how' those beer cartons were sold or the volume of beer I am dealing with.

Can you see that by specifying that I 'Sell pallets of beer cartons' it conjures up a vastly different mental image than if I said, 'Sell schooners of beer.' Selling schooners of beer to me conjures the image of a pub with a beer drinker who could become drunk if I serve them too many beers!

I'm still selling beer, but I'm helping you, the reader, to understand the context by being as specific as I can be in relation to selling beer. I don't sell beer in a pub or club; I most likely sell beer to pubs and clubs!

So my 'Sell products' skill would convert into this skill statement:

> **Sell** (*strong, active verb*) **pallets** (*specific detail*) **of beer cartons** (*the 'what' – our skill, specified by type*).

Now, these skills as written help to paint a fairly good mental picture; but in their current state, the sentences themselves are a bit bland and therefore aren't all that interesting or appealing to hiring managers.

And the solution to this is actually to provide more specific details – specifics that they will find interesting and appealing.

This means, we need to start showing those numbers and quantifiable amounts – which was:

Step 3. Add Numbers and Quantifiable Amounts

Just as earlier leaving out the word 'pallets' didn't adequately describe how my beer cartons were sold, we also don't have much information yet to help hiring manager's to fully understand the volume level of our selling performance.

To do this we need to start adding numbers and quantity amounts.

To demonstrate this, I'll use an example of a receptionist who answers telephone calls.

One receptionist might only answer ten calls a day; another might answer ten an hour; and yet another might have ten phone lines ringing all at once!

It is true that each of those receptionists possess the skill in answers phone calls – but their workload (for completing just that one duty) varies significantly. And it is showing the volume level that sets each of our telephone answering receptionists apart.

Now, I don't know about you, but if I was that last receptionist in particular, I would want the hiring manager to understand and fully appreciate just how busy my role was, compared to my competition who only answered ten calls a day.

But, can you see. Rather than telling them 'I was busy' which is what most jobseekers do, it is better to show how busy your role in answering the phones was. We achieved that by specifying the volume of calls answered over a set period.

Now, it is important to note here that – and this is another secret resume writer's tip I'm going to share – numbers also carry the power, when written in numerical form rather than in word form, to jump out at readers.

That's because numbers are image based, and as we learned in the beginning of this course, our brains see and understand images faster than we can comprehend text, so listing numbers as numbers is a method that causes a skim reading hiring manager to slow down and instead read the detail to ensure they are interpreting the details correctly.

And as we also have learned, getting hiring managers to actually read our resume is one of main resume writing goals.

So, you need to add numbers to your skill statements, wherever and wherever possible, or you are wasting a stellar opportunity, and reducing the effectiveness of your resume.

Earlier I used the example of supervising staff, and we turned my skill statement into:

Supervise kitchen hand and customer service staff members.

Let's examine a Hiring Manager's reading and question-forming behaviour again.

What is the most logical question that they would ask after reading that sentence?

It is: **'How many staff did you supervise?'**

So, answer that question and answer it now. Don't leave them guessing, or save it for an interview. They have asked the question now, so you need to provide them with the answer now, or they might not see your potential suitability so that you are invited to attend an interview to be able to answer that question in person.

So, let's say I managed a small team of 3 kitchen hand and customer service staff members. My skills statement will now look like this:

> **Supervise** (*strong, active verb*) **3** (*quantifiable amount*) **kitchen hand and customer service** (*specific details*) **staff members** (*the 'who'*)

It is only logical that when your numbers closely match what hiring managers are hoping, wanting or expecting to see, then they are going to view you as more suitable than candidates whose numbers are far lesser than their desired number.

But, you will be much more appealing than every candidate that has left them with a volume-level mystery to resolve, as well as every candidate who doesn't show or tell them that they even possess that particular skill. One mismatch between your skill level and employer expectation on its own is unlikely to get your application immediately rejected. It is only when there are multiple mismatches that your application becomes less appealing.

Now, when providing number details think 'quantifiable', and 'proven'

A quantifiable amount is a number – in dollars, time, or rank. 'Proven' means that your referees or supportive documents will be able to back your claim up by attesting to the details accuracy.

What about my selling products skill statement? Could we add numbers to it? Again, yes. We could add both the dollar amount and the time period to make it more specific, so my skill sentence would now look like this:

> **Sell** (*strong, active verb*) **$50,000** (*quantifiable amount in dollars*) **worth of pallets of beer cartons** (*specific detail – of the 'what'*) **each month** (*time frame*)

Can you see how when you read my skill statement you start getting a good sense of what it is that I'm saying I did in my role, and what my performance level was?

Are you finding the information a little more interesting than when I said I sell products?

Step 4, and the last part of the skill statement equation is to add results or specify what the outcome was, because it is these last 2 details which really show hiring managers the implied benefits of what you bring to the role in relation to this skill.

Results and outcomes convince high performance as fact rather than claim. Remember I said at the beginning of this tutorial that we need to write evidence and achievement based sentences?

So, let's say that the result we got for having sold $50,000 worth of beer carton pallets was that I beat my monthly Sales target of $45,000. Our skill statement could be rounded off as reading like this:

> **Sell** (*strong, active verb*) **$50,000** (*quantifiable amount – dollars*) **worth of pallets of beer cartons** (*specific detail – of the 'what'*) **each month** (*time frame + implied benefit to potential employer*) **resulting in consistently exceeding monthly Sales target** (*the result + implied benefit*)

That last part is demonstrating an achievement gained in the workplace. The dollar amounts and specifics are providing the evidence to our claim that we have this skill.

Okay, what about our Supervise staff skill statement? What results or outcomes might I achieve or could be gained?

Let's say, that without proper supervision the staff worked slowly and weren't meeting service deadlines which resulted in customer complaints and poor sales. Rounded off, our skill statement now reads like this:

> **Supervise** (*strong, active verb*) **3** (*quantifiable amount*) **kitchen hand and customer service** (*specific details*) **staff members** (*the 'who'*) **to ensure** (*strong, active verb + goal*) **working safely while meeting food service deadlines and resulting in a reduction in customer complaints and an increase in daily sales** (*the result + implied benefit to the employer - responsibility*).

While you write your skill statements, use the information you wrote into workbook activities WB09 Volume Amounts (colour four) and WB10 Results and Outcomes (Colour five) to compare the volume amounts you dealt with against what the employers have stated they are looking for.

Don't lie about any of your numbers or results; what you are aiming to do is address those numbers and results that are important to the employers and also work out where you fit on the scale of volume amounts and results – so you can plan before an interview if they differ-sizeably how you could address the difference if the employer enquires about them, especially when your levels are less than what they are looking at.

So as you work, make a note in the space provided at WB09 and WB10 whether you match, achieved higher or achieved lower than their expectation. The way I do this is to use the equals sign (=) when there is a match, and an Up Arrow (⬆) to indicate it is higher, and a Down Arrow (⬇) to indicate when it is lower – as this enables me to see an area of weakness visually.

Now, if you follow how I have built my skill statements, the sentence will read positively. This leads us to our last step in the process, which was:

Step 5 – Ensure targeted, positive language is used

I cannot reiterate strongly enough that jobseekers must sell themselves in a positive manner throughout the job search process, not just while resume writing.

I have assessed thousands of resume over the last 10 years, and I absolutely amazed by how many jobseekers and how frequently they incorporate what they can't do, what they are limited by, and what they don't want into their applications.

Those negative elements – the 'can't', the limit and the 'don't want' – do not belong in a resume. Ever.

Actually, take them as a clear sign that you have the wrong mindset that gets your applications rejected.

Now, I realise that many of you might not have worked in a paid position previously, but that does not matter. A skill is a skill, regardless of how or where you gained it.

I have never worked as a professional driver at all. But I do know how to drive a manual vehicle, and have a licence. In a previous job, one of the skills that the employer was looking for was people who drove and had a car – because the position involved going out to meet employers occasionally. There were about 10 staff that worked in the office – including the Management, and somehow after transfers and internal reshuffling, they ended up with no staff member at that branch having a driver's licence or car. And I got the job, over the only other candidate they were interested in because I had a car and driver's licence and the other candidate didn't.

So, if you haven't held a job before, you:

1. Still have skills, and
2. Can therefore turn those skills into compelling skill statements.

Just like people who have had a job in the past. The only difference is that you will use non-workplace specifics to show how you gained them. You will still be able to get specific and add numbers and results.

Okay. Are you ready to start transforming your raw skills list into compelling skill statements?

Remember, the equation to use is:

Strong Active Verb + Specific Supportive Details + Results = Compelling Skill Statement

The 5 steps you need to follow are:

Step 1. Choose a Skill.
Step 2. Choose an appropriate Action Word
Step 3. Add Numbers and Quantifiable Amounts
Step 4. Add Results and Outcomes
Step 5. Ensure targeted, positive language is used

The question you need to ask yourself for each skill is: Could I be more specific?

And, once you have completed writing your sentence, ask: Does this sentence paint a strong mental picture of my performance and capability?

You can now head return to your Student Workbook and complete activity WB13. When you have done this, you will have completed the hardest part of writing your resume!

As always, thank you for watching. And I will see you in the next tutorial.

WB13 – Transform Core Skills into Skill Statements

Skill 1	
Action Word:	
Specifics:	
Result / Benefit:	

Skill 2	
Action Word:	
Specifics:	
Result / Benefit:	

Skill 3	
Action Word:	
Specifics:	
Result / Benefit:	

Skill 4	
Action Word:	
Specifics:	
Result / Benefit:	

Skill 5	
Action Word:	
Specifics:	
Result / Benefit:	

Skill 6	
Action Word:	
Specifics:	
Result / Benefit:	

Skill 7	

Action Word:	
Specifics:	
Result / Benefit:	

Skill 8	
Action Word:	
Specifics:	
Result / Benefit:	

Skill 9	
Action Word:	
Specifics:	
Result / Benefit:	

Skill 10	
Action Word:	
Specifics:	
Result / Benefit:	

TUTORIAL 08. CORE SKILLS Section

This is video 8 of 8 for Lesson: Core Skills section.

Welcome back. You are still in Lesson 04 Core Skills section in the Develop Your Resume Content module for the Write a Functional Resume course. This is the eighth tutorial for this lesson.

In the previous tutorial, I taught you how to use a compelling skill statement equation to turn the raw list of skills we wrote down in the student workbook activity WB06, to head on over to workbook activity WB13 to write your own fully fleshed out skill statements.

I hope you were able to successfully complete that activity.

Now, in this last tutorial for Lesson 04 Core Skills, I want to discuss that although you just turned your entire list of skills into skill statements, you may have ended up with far more skill statements than you will need to use in this section.

Ideally, the Core Skills section should only include no more than 8 Skill Statements if you are creating a one-page resume and no more than 12 if you create a two-page resume. Because you are creating a Functional resume, your resume should not end up more than 2 pages in length.

So, if you have more than 8 or 12 skill statements, I only want you to include the skills that you identified as being the most important to the greatest number of employers – so you may need to go back and check your marked up job advertisements to work this out, if necessary.

But, hang on to the extra skill statements that you leave off, because if you find that employers are not responding as you hoped after you have trialled your new resume for a while, then you might take out some of what you had put in and put in some of what you had left out to mix things up a little, and trial that for a set period – because you should always refresh your resume at least every three months to test out what employers respond to best.

And, you could always use the skills that have not been included in your resume as possible skills you could mention within your cover letter instead – so having done more than what you need is never a waste of time in having done that.

So, you can now return to your Student Workbook and add your Top 8 Core Skills skill statements to your Functional Resume Master Worksheet. I am really proud of how well you are progressing. And I'm delighted to tell you, you've actually got most of the hard work done and out of the way now, and are ready to power your way towards the finish line. So, with that wonderful thought in mind, I'll see you in the next lesson.

LESSON 05.

PERSONAL PROFILE SECTION

LESSON INTRO

Congratulations on your great progress in this course.

You are now up to Lesson 05 Personal Profiles in the Develop Your Resume Content module of the Write a Functional Resume course.

A Personal Profile section is the second Summary Information component that we include in our Functional resume. (The first was our Core Skills section which we covered in the last lesson.)

Now, I know I already covered some of the Personal Profile section during the Core Skills section tutorials, but it is important this section gets its own lesson and that you are clear and can include the section in your resume. So in this lesson's video tutorials, we will look at the same five key areas that we have done for each of the previous sections, only this time specifically related to Personal Profiles:

Those key areas are:

1. What a Personal Profile section is
2. What a typical Personal Profile section looks like
3. What alternatives - if any - you can use,
4. How to decide on details to include in your Personal Profile section, and
5. How to write those details so that they are likely to be interesting to a Hiring Manager.

So, when you are ready, join me in the first tutorial for this lesson.

TUTORIAL 01. PERSONAL PROFILE Section

This is video 1 of 5 for Lesson: Personal Profile section.

In our previous lesson covering the Core Skills section tutorials, I discussed a number of things that apply to the Personal Profile section also.

Those core points included that:

- The 2 sections work in partnership with each other,
- Both sections are just bullet listings, and
- There are 2 methods that you could use to flesh the bullet listings out, which were writing lists using sentence or word (or short phrase list) form

I discussed too:

- the importance of our resume being less about us and more about the job,
- the need to answer Hiring Managers most fundamental initial questions in our resume, and
- the secret to doing that is to show not tell and this writing in sentence form is what makes us gain a competitive edge, 'stand out' and impress them, especially when we get specific on the details, because it enables
- the hiring manager to picture us using our skills and therefore enables them to better mentally match us up against their wants and needs, and
- that we can't ever please all employers all of the time, but we can sure aim to cause as many as we can to view us in a favourable light.

All of that applies to our Personal Profile section just as much as it did for our Core Skills section. Actually, I would argue that it is even more important now – which I'll discuss later.

For now, the only real difference is that whereas our Core Skills section was all about our skills for the job and our ability to answer their initial hiring questions, our Personal Profile section is all about your attributes for the role and answering their secondary hiring questions now that the hiring manager has reached our highly desirable wanting to know, "What is this applicant like?"

Because we have already fully covered all the WHY aspects back in the Core Skill section lessons, I won't re-explain those WHY's during this lesson; though, I will mention the important aspects again as we progress through this lesson's tutorials.

So please forgive any part that may sound repetitive as we go through this lesson. I have lots of new things to share with you too, so let's get started on the Personal Profile section specific learning, shall we?

What a Personal Profile section is

I'll start by re-clarifying that the Personal Profile section should not be confused with the similar sounding Personal Details section which we previous dealt with in lesson 1 – that's where we examined which of our private and sensitive personal and contact information belongs and doesn't belong in our resume.

No, the Personal Profile section is a whole other section entirely, one that is essential for us to include in our resume because it is the second half of what makes a functional resume functional. And specifically, it is a section dedicated to listing our unique personal attributes so that it shows how we match the personal natured aspects the employer is looking for.

What a typical Personal Profile section looks like

Many people who write a resume for themself (without really knowing what to do) make the mistake of using word or short phrase list form as their way of fleshing out a Personal Profile type section.

A typical listing therefore ends up looking similar to this:

- Team Player
- Punctual
- Reliable
- Fast Learner
- Organised
- Hard working
- Friendly
- Able to follow instructions
- Attention to detail

As I've discussed throughout this course, you never want to create a 'typical' section that the 95% majority do, as this is the fastest way to cause your application to be rejected along with theirs. So, we are not going to create a list that looks like that list above in our resume.

However, I will tell you the reason underlying why those resumes are rejected.

Those types of lists are the starting point, not the ending point.

Listed in isolation like that in a functional resume, those words don't mean anything. They are simply a shopping list of words on paper – a cliché listing of common resume-related words.

They are cliché because they are trite and lack original thought.

In particular, they turn hiring managers off because:

- they add no value
- do not show the applicants benefits or uniqueness
- are boring and unimaginative to read
- are subjective in nature, and
- ultimately are unprovable (or, are disputable) claims

Generally what happens is employers' indicate within their job advertisement or the position description that they are looking for someone with specific personal characteristics, and the jobseeker responds by listing those traits back at the employer in the above word or short phrase list form – a response, by the way, which is called Rehashing the Job Advertisement.

This practice of rehashing the job advertisement is widespread and mostly used by the lazy, uneducated or low-skilled. The practice is the unimpressive way to address the employer's criteria for the decision makers, and is therefore one of the first things hiring managers look for as their means for deciding 'we can reject this application' when they have hundreds to sort through.

Why?

As we've discussed plenty of times and at the risk of my sledge-hammering the point, our details have to mean something to the employer in order for the specifics to be interesting or appealing.

If the employer can reject applications quickly, it frees them up to spend more time on the applications of those who are potentially suitable rather than wasting time on those who aren't up to scratch.

So we want (and need) to emulate what the professional resume writers and successful jobseekers do.

The only way to make our details meaningful to the hiring manager is to provide the context behind them, and to make that context unique in its expression.

Which just means: ***write custom-written personal attribute sentences.***

*Laughing*You saw that coming, didn't you.

I'll show you how not to rehash the job advertisement but still convey these attributes later on in this lesson.

Okay, so we've covered that on a zoomed in on viewpoint, we need to write Personal Attribute statements for our Personal Profile section listing; and I've hinted that we will do more than just create personal attribute statements.

Now, we'll look at the big picture viewpoint again.

What alternatives – if any – you can use

Like for the Core Skills section there are no alternatives. Once again, you simply choose to either include these sections in your functional resume or you leave one or both out.

And, you already know the reasons why I believe you would be mad to decide to leave either out. If you don't remember the whys, go back and rewatch the Core Skills lesson tutorials.

So that is the 'what alternatives' part done.

Now, before we move on to the deciding on the details to include in our Personal Profile section and how to write the details – and if you've flipped through the workbook at all you'll have already figured out that we will be handling this section slightly to the Core Skills section – ooh, that was another hint [laugh]. But first, I want to discuss our having switched the Core Skills and Personal sections around.

Impact of Switching the Core Skills and Personal Profile sections around

The reason I suggested you switch the two sections around, if you recall, is so that the information is presented in the same logical order that hiring managers generally assess the person's potential suitability – to prevent the hiring manager to have to jump back and forth all around your resume (which they don't like doing and can cause them to reject applications if they have to do this excessively) to find information and get answers to the questions they want to know.

What I didn't specify in the last lesson was that by switching the two sections around, your Core Skills section now falls into the area I have called the PRRE – which you will remember is the Prime Resume Real Estate – which it wouldn't have been in otherwise. This is a good thing.

But in doing this, it means that our Personal Profile section – especially if we have included a Career Objective section – most likely will now be located outside of the PRRE.

I bring this up because I wanted to tell you that it is okay if our Personal Profile section is not in the PRRE. Employers won't be expecting this, of course, but our doing this is not necessarily a bad thing.

It is impossible to fit everything into the PRRE. We have placed, and the majority of hiring managers should appreciate that we have done this, our most important details already filling up that area. Because we've shown them we understand and care about what is important to them.

And whether they become consciously aware of it or not, they will note that extra effort has been put into this resume and application – and that is a positive judgement we are happy for them to make about us because it will go a long way to making us look better than our competition.

So, we've now covered what the Personal Profile section is, what a typical Personal Profile listing looks like, that we have no alternatives to this section on a big picture view, and that it is okay if our section doesn't end up in the PRRE.

In the next tutorial, we'll look at this section from the hiring manager's perspective again so we can get on with deciding on the details to include in this section, and then how to address your attributes effectively.

So, as always, thank you so much for watching and participating so actively in this course. And I'll see you in the next tutorial.

TUTORIAL 02. PERSONAL PROFILE Section

This is video 2 of 5 for Lesson: Personal Profile section.

Thank you for rejoining me. This is Tutorial 02 in Lesson 05 the Personal Profile section in the Develop Your Content module of the Create a Functional Resume course.

In the previous tutorial, I recapped the important aspects of the Personal Profile section that we covered in the Core Skills section lesson and then looked at what the Personal Profile section is, what a typical Personal Profile section looks like and that it will be positioned after the core skills section and is most likely to fall outside of the Prime Resume Real Estate.

I'm all for making our sections and specifics the strongest, most effective and compelling as we can possibly make them; and as we've done before, we must first understand what is going on for the hiring manager reviewing applications so we can do that.

Therefore, this tutorial is about how we can keep a hold of the hiring manager's interest now that we have gained it.

It's time to put our Hiring Managers hat on again

So far our hiring manager has picked up (or in modern times more likely to have opened on screen) a resume. Because of our visual processing speed and power, before any single word comes into focus, they have already mentally noted:

- the layout to know if this document will be easy to read
- that they've been able to mentally tick off whether all the expected sections are present, and
- know whether they will be able to contact this person if they want to know more about them or decide they want to meet them.

Or not.

Now, because we read and write using English, readers naturally start at the top left most corner of the page, and navigate reading and skim reading progress in a left to right downward sweeping motion.

Our hiring manager reads in the same way. The important difference to note here is that while their eyes are sweeping the page, they are on the lookout for the specific key words they are hoping, wanting or expecting to see. It is finding those keywords that help them to decide if they want to stop to read any specific text or just continue skimming down the page to mentally tick off other areas of interest.

If any of the preceding sections or details has indeed grabbed their hiring attention – which we have done our absolute best to ensure happens, haven't we? and can assume they will indeed find words of interest – the hiring manager now has a clear idea of what you can do and will have made an initial value judgement that we either outrightly or closely match what they are after, so far in our application.

So, the first thought that goes through their head from their favourable read and matching us up to their skill needs and requirements, is something like, 'I might have a winner here'.

Then their secondary thoughts come into formation. Usually they are questions, which go something like:

- *'Oooh, who is this applicant?'* And, *'I wonder what they are like as an employee?'*

Well, that's generally how I reacted each time I discovered a resume that stood out against the 95% majority boring me.

Now, I want to digress for a moment to get you to notice four specific things here.

Firstly, I said the hiring manager's thoughts are something like, 'I might have a winner here,' not, 'We have a winner here.'

This is because the Hiring Manager has not made up their mind about your suitability yet; they are still just exploring the possibility that you might be the right person.

So, well done. At least they haven't decided to reject your application like they've done for the other – do you remember the percentage? That's right, the other 95% they rejected the moment they reached their natural stopping point.

And, to avoid having this happen to you too – because there is still a chance this could happen at any time throughout the rest of the hiring process – you now need to continue to show them your suitability. Which we will get to in a short while.

The second thing I want you to notice is although they have seen and noted your Personal Details are present, up until now they haven't bothered to get to know the applicants names. Now, is the point where they are likely to want to know this, so quickly flick their eyes back up to the top of the page so they can read and comprehend what this applicants name is. Before immediately flicking their focus back to where they had just stopped on.

The third thing I want you to notice is now that they have answered their question, 'who is this applicant?' they will incorporate that new knowledge of the applicants name into their asking their next question – so they are more likely to think, 'I wonder what applicants name is like as an employee?'

If this is the case, you've just successfully pulled the hiring manager in one more step closer towards liking you. That's what happens when a person uses another person's name like this. So even though you don't know – and probably never will – the hiring manager is doing this, you are nailing your application!

The fourth and final thing I wanted you to notice about this is that I said, 'what applicants name is like as an employee.' I intentionally avoided saying, 'what applicants name is like as a person.'

I did that for a reason.

You see, you – and even hiring managers – might think the hiring manager wants to know about who you are as a person, and may even use that specific wording when formulating or verbalising that thought, but in reality, the heart of what the hiring manager is really exploring or what they are actually trying you on for size is, 'What is applicants name likely to be like as an employee?'

Some parts of who you are as a person and what you are like outside of employment is not relevant to the job, and never will be. But – and I know my saying this upsets many jobseekers – a lot of who you are as a person and what you are like outside of employment is. And it is those aspects that will immediately impact upon your employability with this particular employer reviewing your application.

It is important to remember here that the hiring manager is not assessing you with the view of becoming your best friend, or entering into a personal relationship. This is why things like your sexual preferences are irrelevant and inappropriate.

The hiring manager is assessing your candidacy for business purposes, for filling their specific vacancy needs.

So, they do have to like you.

They do have to feel that they can trust you, that you could do the job, do it well and that you won't cause them any problems – now or in the future.

So ultimately, they do have to believe that you will fit into their business and culture, hassle free.

And, they achieve this through making judgements.

I can almost hear the roar of protests from some jobseekers, but please hear with me out on this, and be open to understanding my point.

We all make judgements in situations we come across in our daily lives; that is a fundamental element of human nature that protects us from harm, fulfils our basic physical and psychological needs, and ensures our continued survival in this world.

Please accept this fact, rather than fighting it: when you send an employer a job application, you are actually asking them to make a value judgement about you – based on the information you have provided them.

And whether you agree with them doing so or not, the employer will make a judgement – and that judgement will only ever be the one that best protects their business from harm, fulfils their physical and psychological needs so that they ensure their business continues to survive within the business world.

Don't expect them to do or be any different to what you do yourself.

It is your job, as the party asking another party to make a judgement, to enable them to reach the very value judgement you want them to make.

Within the constraints of their job advertisement (or other means of letting jobseekers know they are open to receive applications) they have told you – upfront – want they are looking for. You must, within the constraints of your job application, address what they are looking for and show them why they should make the value judgement that matches the one you desire; that is, they should see your suitability and therefore consider you further.

If your application is rejected during their initial skim read review, then the single reason for their having come to that premature decision is because for whatever reason, you failed to give this particular employer cause to make your desired value judgement that you are the most suitable. The proof they need wasn't in your application.

It is the same reason why the other 95% of applications are rejected; they haven't proven to the employer they should consider the applicant further.

Now, a second fundamental human behaviour is that we won't blindly believe in something from what someone tells us; we are more inclined to believe as a result of:

1. What we observe directly our own self, or
2. Enquiring to an independent person or using an independent resource

When we are looking to purchase a product or service, we will go through a company that we used in the past and trust will continue to meet our needs; and if we haven't used the company previously, it's why we check out reviews and testimonials.

Back to our applications, the 'observing for our own self' part will come when the hiring manager reads our resume and makes judgements based on from what they see and decide.

The 'enquiring or using an independent resource' part is their contacting our referees and or carrying out their pre-employment fact checking tasks.

Educate the Employer

We have to remember – because it is so easy to forget this – is that the receiver of our job applications doesn't know anything about us; so our job is always to educate them by showing them the employability relevant parts to your personality, behaviours and what makes you tick as key attention-grabbing points for this section.

And again, we must balance this with not trying to tell them everything about ourselves, or we risk un-selling ourselves instead. The tipping point between too much and too little is the hardest part for most jobseekers.

Educating the employer comes down to show not tell again, doesn't it. Which we have covered the whys already.

The balance tipping point comes down to our deciding what details we cover or don't cover. And this is the next section in our learning agenda.

How to decide on details to include in your Personal Profile section

As you have probably already guessed, we are doing our best to be smart and purposeful in how we approach writing our resume, and that means we will use the attributes that we gleaned from the job advertisements as our starting point for deciding on which specific attributes we will include in our Personal Profile section.

But pay attention, because I have a few more tips and techniques I want to share and discuss before we start on completing any workbook activities.

The Hiring Manager Hat again

We haven't quite finished looking at things from the hiring manager's perspective yet. And we need to do that.

So far we've discussed that the hiring manager has liked most or everything so far for them to be interested in us as potentially suitable to explore further. But, before they are ready to take that all important next step forward that we want too, in perhaps contacting us or passing our application to the next decision maker, they have one last curiosity to resolve – that is to want to learn a little bit more about you, specifically.

I remind you that they may use or think words like, 'want to see a bit more about who you are as a person' but as I already discussed, they really only want to continue 'trying you on for size' as a potential employee.

So, while they may have a few 'you' focused questions, they are in fact fully business oriented ones.

The main question they are really attempting to answer, at its heart, is: 'what is this person likely to be like as an employee for us?' Because they will never truly gain a fully accurate idea of what you will be like until a few months in, when you are working for them. We're all on our best behaviour in the early stages of a new relationship. So in the meantime, the hiring manager is only trying to figure out what you are likely to be like.

And this curiosity prompts them to ask themselves more questions: secondary hiring questions that are you-focused. In effect, a darkened stage bursts into light, with all the spotlights firmly directed onto you – the central act.

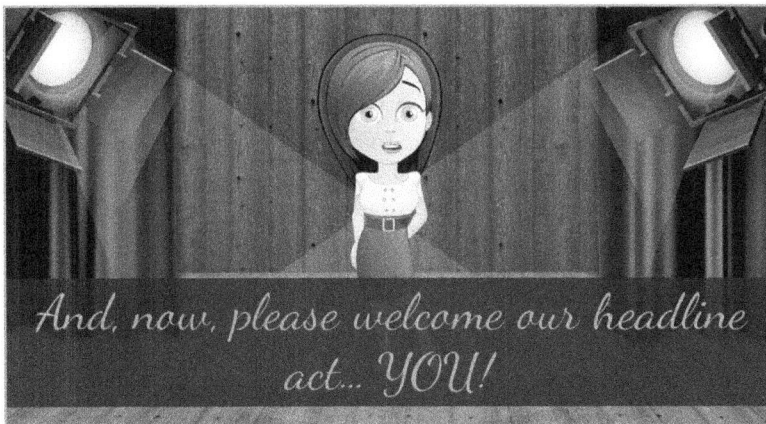

And, now, please welcome our headline act... YOU!

So the hiring manager's questions will be something along the lines of:

- Were they any good?
- Were they reliable?
- What was their behaviour and attitude like?
- Are there any problems I need to be wary of? Any issues I need to be concerned about?

And the questions will come quickly, one after the other like that.

So, like I have encouraged throughout this entire course, we need to answer these questions now while the hiring manager is asking them, not hold out for 'later' because a later opportunity may never come.

Answers can fall outside of this section

Now, it is super important to note here that some of the answers are answered outside of the Personal Profile section.

For example, were they reliable, and are there any problems I need to be wary of are oftentimes answers the hiring managers mostly have to guess at.

And, the clues and answers are scattered throughout the entire resume – either from what you intentionally chose to include in your resume, or the details you decided to leave out – not just in the Personal Profile section.

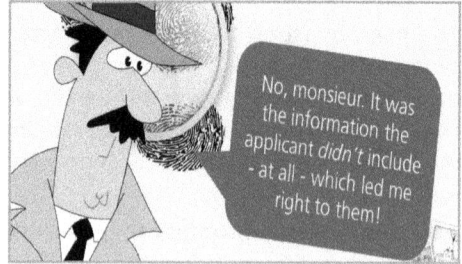

So even though you are creating the sections of your resume one section at a time, you've got to remember that each of the sections are part of a whole; and that rarely is anything ever taken in complete isolation.

Because we want the judgements we are asking the hiring manager to make about us to match our intentions, it is so easy for them to reach a different judgement, and the best way for learners to understand something is when they model it, I'm going to put you in the hot seat for a minute.

I want you to look at the resume on screen for a moment. The scenario I'm going to take

WORK HISTORY

January 2010 – April 2010	Coke-Cola Company Ltd
April 2010 – May 2010	Waterman Wholesalers
May 2010 – August 2010	AGC Holdings Ltd
August 2010 – August 2010	Pickerings Ltd
August 2010 – November 2010	Hays Wholesale Distributions
November 2010 – February 2011	Newhams Ice Cream
February 2011 – June 2011	Monnow Australia
June 2011 – July 2011	ADB Transport Pty Ltd
July 2011 – October 2011	Kings Wholesale Distribution Ltd
October 2011 – December 2011	TJ's Offset Printing Distribution
January 2012 – February 2012	Coke-Cola Company Ltd
March 2012 – August 2012	Adams Express Transport

you through is from a real past client I inherited onto my caseload when he had been unemployed for 4 months – only I've fabricated the resume for you.

If you look at his Work History section, what do you notice?

In case you can't tell, I'll point it out. He has listed 12 different positions over a 3 year period.

By my mental calculations, that equates to him lasting – on average – about 3 months in each position, yeah?

For this exercise you are the hiring manager, and you are considering him for a role. Everything else on this applicant's resume up until this point has been what you are after, so you're thinking 'maybe I have a winner here.' In other words, you believe he has the skills you want and now you are looking at what he might be like as an employee.

So my next question to you is this:

What was YOUR immediate reaction, what was the impression you got when you learned about his having held so many jobs?

What I'm asking here is:

Do you believe that there may be problems in relation to his employment? Or does that many jobs seem perfectly reasonable to you?

I want you to take a moment to write down your answer in the student workbook – activity 7.1. I want you to commit to your opinion by ticking yes or no to that question, and then, in a couple of words, explain why you ticked yes or no.

I'll give you a few moments to do this...

Activity

WB14– Wearing the Hiring Manager Hat

| 5.2 | Do you believe that there may be problems in relation to his being an employee? Or, does that many jobs seem perfectly reasonable to you? | ☐ Yes - may be a problem
☐ No - it is fine |

	Briefly explain why you believe what you do...	

Okay, what did you come up with? Yes or No?

By the way, there is no right or wrong answer here. Whatever you ticked and wrote down as your reasons is completely valid.

My guess though, is that like many hiring managers', a large number of you went with, 'Yes, there could be a problem' within his past employment.

And your reason for coming to that conclusion would be something like 12 jobs over 3 years is excessive so there could well be a problem with his workplace performance, attitude or behaviour for you to be wary about.

Now, while you and I may be curious about this client and will get to the why this was the case in a moment, most hiring managers I know would be unlikely to want this explained to them but whatever the reason is they wouldn't want to inherit it, especially if they have other applicants they could consider. And I fully acknowledge here that the decision to consider the person further would depend on many factors.

I had a yes, maybe and no pile and hardly ever revisited the 'maybe' pile once I was done reviewing applications. And I never revisited the 'no' pile because I trusted my gut instincts and the value judgement I made the first time round was the right one.

The main reason I didn't revisit my 'maybe' pile was almost always because I had enough resumes left in my 'yes' pile – my task had been to cut the number of applications down in size. So, at the end of reviewing applications – because I generally went through them all in one sitting – if I had more than 2 applications in my 'yes' pile, I felt justified to end consideration for the rest.

So back to the client here.

When I first saw his resume, like you and every employer he sent applications to, I didn't know anything else about him, except what was in his resume.

And, without any further information to lead me to make a different value judgement,

I'm not ashamed to admit I assumed that there was a potential problem; so I looked forward to meeting him so I could work out how I could lead him towards addressing the employment barrier he was facing.

And I soon learned two things.

Firstly, he had had no success with any of his application in that 4 month period. Like me, it seemed employers too felt there was a potential problem and were unwilling to take the risk of finding out firsthand what that problem is. If there were employers who would be prepared to take a risk, he hadn't sent an application to them.

Secondly, because I only had a part of the story, employers and my own self were making the wrong value judgement. Actually, I'll correct that. We were each making the value judgement we had been presented with. It was his application that led us to make the opposite value judgement to his intention.

Now, I'll give you more information about this client and see if that makes any difference to those of you who like me viewed his 12 positions as a potential problem we don't know about.

The missing details are: this client had successfully been employed for the full 3 year period.

What? You might be asking.

Yes, he had been employed the entire time by one employer – a recruitment company. Who assigned him to host employers to complete short term assignments.

The crucial piece of information he had not conveyed properly was that he was continuously employed by the one recruitment company. His listing the individual host employers he had been assigned to was the cause of our misjudgement. By halfway through our first consultation, I had learned that he had never actually been out of work for any longer than one week – because the host employers and the recruitment company managing him loved him.

So, why was he unemployed now? The recruitment company closed down, and the short term assignment he was hosted out to, came to an end, as expected. He had started sending out his resume a month before he finished up, so had been actively looking for work for five months, not four.

He completed short term assignments at different host employers. He was employed by the recruitment company, not the individual host employers he was assigned to. Although he didn't get paid for the few days or weeks between assignments, he was actually never out of work for any longer than 1 week – because the host employers and the recruitment company loved him.

So the points here are:

1. the judgements hiring managers make about applicants about their performance, attitude and behaviours aren't just gleaned from this section,
2. just as you had to make a judgement, so too will each hiring manager who receives an application from you have to make one, and
3. the client did not have to write 'reliable' anywhere in his resume just then for us to consider him reliable and hassle-free now that we have a clearer, more accurate picture about his employability.

Just so you know, the simple fix – which had an immediate impact on his jobsearch results – was I adjusted his resume to show that he was employed by the one employer – the recruitment company paying his wages – and that the companies he worked at (which were reputable and desirable) were just host employers.

This particular client was hired within a week after that single change to his resume.

So, that was an example of not providing enough information to lead employers too view us favourably, now to briefly address the effects if we tell them too much information about ourselves.

Balancing this with not telling them too much

In almost every resume I have ever had to fix up though, one of the first things I've had to remove is excess information relating to the person.

Too many jobseekers tell employers far too much about who they are as a person. But, instead of those details selling their best skills and employability to the hiring manager, it actually achieves the opposite in un-selling them. Because they come across as being desperate or too salesy.

There are many reasons underlying jobseekers providing too much information, and it is usually something like:

- Lack of confidence a person has about themself
- Lack of resume writing knowledge or the skills to carry it out
- Approaching resume writing or jobsearching from the wrong mindset
- Not understanding what hiring managers want and need
- Poor self-marketing skills
- Blindness to the impact their words and message has on the receiver
- Overcompensating in response to repeated rejection in desperate attempt to turn things around or try something new or different

When we completed our job advertisement 'side activity' at the beginning of the Core Skills section lesson, we developed a list of the personal attributes that employers have told us are important to them. So, our decision about what attributes to address has been made for us.

But, we are not going to just dive in and start turning our personal attributes into personal attribute statements.

So, meet me in the next tutorial, and we'll get started on developing our resume content again.

As always, thank you for watching, see you in the next tutorial.

TUTORIAL 03. PERSONAL PROFILE Section

This is video 3 of 5 for Lesson: Personal Profile section.

Thank you for rejoining me. This is Tutorial 03 in Lesson 05 the Personal Profile section in the Develop Your Content module of the Create a Functional Resume course.

In the previous tutorial, I got you to dive in deeper into wearing the hiring manager's hat as we discussed the impact of the personal side to 'what is this applicant likely to be like as an employee' comes from the entire resume not just this section.

So we are now up to the final stage of how to write those details so that they are likely to be interesting to the hiring manager.

As I told you back in the Core Skills section, we must write evidence and achievement based statements rather than claiming specific skills or attributes in short form.

When we write using the skill or personal attribute statement formula we are providing evidence and achievements to back our claims. And those can then be further confirmed later by our Referees and References.

There are 2 ways for us to handle our attributes so we get them into our resume. These are, by either:

1. Writing dedicated personal attribute statements, or
2. Blending personal attribute (where relevant and appropriate) into one of your existing skill statements.

Let's look at both methods, and work out which is the better method to use.

Writing a dedicated Personal Attribute Statement

Now, for this method you actually already know what to do. You just use the same equation and process that you followed to build your Skill Statement for your Core Skills section; that is, follow the Skill Statement equation and go through each of the five steps to incrementally build up compelling statements – writing in layers and backing your claims up with strong and interesting evidence and achievement based supportive details as you work.

The only differences between how you did this for your skills to what you would do for your attributes are:

- step one now reads as Choose an Attribute instead of Choose a Skill, and
- you work your way through the list of attributes recorded in WB08 instead of the

skills listed in activity WB06.

You even still ask the same 2 questions that we asked in relation to when we wrote out our skills: 'Can I be more specific?' as you are building up your sentences, and 'Does this sentence paint a strong mental picture?' once you've finished.

Now, this is a good method for addressing the lesser important personal attributes.

But, there is a better method for addressing the higher important personal attributes, and that is to blend key attributes into the skill statements you've written.

Why is blending attributes better?

Well, like the Career Objective section, many hiring managers don't bother to read what an applicant writes in this section. While they are almost guaranteed to not bother at all reading typical lists that use word or short phrase list form, hiring managers will still be sceptical about what the jobseeker tells them about themself in relation to their personal aspects. It's not like they aren't sceptical about our skills, it's just their scepticism isn't as strong for skills compared to what we say are our attributes.

Again, they are more inclined to make judgements from their own observations of the interactions they have with you in written, verbal and visual forms than to blindly believe anything we actually say in writing or in person.

Creating our resume is our saying things in writing, so straight away it will be hard to convince them we have the attributes they are looking for because they can't observe us in the same way they can do if we attend in person.

Just as some hiring managers read Career Objective statements and others don't, the same is true for Personal Profile sections – it is one of the reasons why I got you to move this section to after the core skills section, because we don't want 2 sections they might not look positioned next to each other, or taking up our entire prime resume real estate.

Now, if it is true any particular hiring manager will just skip over this section, then as a result of that unwanted act we will have lost our chance to show them we not only have the skills they are looking for, but have the right personal attributes too. And we still need to address our personal attributes because they want us to – they are in the job advertisements to enable us to 1. Consider our suitability to their requirements and 2. Address those requirements.

And that's why we are lucky writing personal attribute statements are not our only choice, and why blending them into our skill statement is the better choice of the two.

We know hiring managers like and want to learn about our skills, and are therefore unlikely to skip past reading our Core Skills section. So it makes perfect sense for us to leverage this to our advantage by incorporating some of our most important attributes into our skill statements while and where we have their captive-attention.

And again though, we don't want to just sledgehammer our details at them; no, we want to subtly slip them in and make them look like they are a fully meant to be part of the skill statement too. That their presence is both logical and appropriate.

So, before I send you off to complete any workbook activities, let's look at how we can strategically and creatively blend personal attributes into our skill statements.

Blending Attributes into our Skill Statements

The best way to teach you this, of course, is with another example.

I'll use another real client's skill statement which they sent through to me when asking me for help to make his resume a bit more effective.

Now, it is important to note here that the skill statement we improved does not fully follow the equation I got you to use previously, but it does appropriately and adequately paint an accurate picture and addresses a key criterion the client needed to address – and as I've mentioned before we don't ever fix what ain't broke if we can avoid it. We provided you with the equation simply to help you get started with writing statements; we are not claiming the equation is the 'be all or end all' for how to make the details interesting, meaningful and effective.

So, with that in mind, this client's original skill statement read like this:

- Deactivate security system, perform security checks and allow staff entry each day so that they can carry out required pre-operational tasks like getting set up, booting up computers and opening applications ready for branch opening.

And in a Personal Attributes list he had written using word or short phrase form:

- Punctual
- Reliable

... Because those 2 personal attributes were what every employer for the type of work he sought stated consistently very early on within their job advertisements was a key requirement.

So, rather than rehashing the job advertisement back at the employer like he had done, I worked with him to look for natural ways with which to demonstrate a time or circumstance where it was essential for him to be reliable and punctual in the workplace.

And bingo, I quickly spied that particular skill statement of his above and knew that with just a few simple words added, or what I call 'tweaking', we could not only achieve describing what he did, but would fully and adequately be able to build in those two personal attributes at the same time.

So, compare the skill statement he originally wrote against how I revised it to read:

- Arrived to work on time to deactivate security s system, perform security checks and allow staff entry each do so that they can carry out pre-operational tasks like getting set up, booting up computers and opening applications.

I only added six words, I didn't remove any.

So, what did I add?

I'll give you a few moments to work it out for yourself.

What has been added?

I added the words 'arrived to work on time to...' at the beginning of his sentence. That's all.

But can you see how those six words – in particular the words arrived and on time – not only show punctuality and reliability in action rather than tell them, it also:

1. Makes his entire skill sentence and the responsibility in relation to this skill clearer for the reader,
2. It addresses his need to be reliable and punctual or else it would negatively affect his co-workers, and
3. Simultaneously, it kept the sentence starting off on a strong, action word?

Do you think it might also contribute to a hiring manager judging that he might be a team member too?

Thank about it for a moment. He has the keys and security codes. He would have to arrange for someone to do this daily task if for any reason he would be absent, either planned or unplanned days off – or, the entire office would be affected not being able to get inside the building.

Now, I used the words 'arrived at work on time to...' to convey those personal attributes, but you should keep true to how you write and speak, so you might come up with a different way of conveying the same thing.

Can you see, though, that with a little bit of thought and intentional effort, it is possible to find simple, interesting and compelling ways to blend important attributes in?

For example, you might write 'commence on time to...'

The point here is to use the English language so that your sentences are personalised and custom-written. Grab a dictionary and thesaurus to help you, if you need to.

WB15 Workbook Activity

Now, what you probably found with your list for this section is that what you have written in WB08 looks similar to the typical Personal Attribute listings. That is, all you have is cliché words or short phrases.

It is okay if employers have done this. The important part is for us not to list them like that, isn't it?

So, we are going to do another workbook activity.

In the space provided in the Student Workbook we will now complete activity WB15.

There are 3 steps involved for this activity.

Step 1. Is to examine your list at WB08 and check that all the most important attributes employer are looking for are on your list – that you don't have any important attributes missing, so your list is thorough and complete – so that you can address them.

It also means striking out any attribute that you feel don't you have, or a weak on (because remember, we need to be honest in our resume – though, I generally find most people feel they have the attributes needed even if they don't feel they have the skills.)

Step 2. Is to rewrite your list of Personal Attributes recorded from WB08 into the space provided at WB15, so that your attributes list is in order of most important to the employer to least important.

We did this for our skills in the last lesson too. If you have any problems deciding on what is most important to least important, then please use the job advertisements as a guide and or seek the assistance from a family member or friend.

Step 3. Is to reword those personal attributes so that they will be personalised and custom written.

In other words, we are going to treat our list of attributes as though they are concepts, and write down how we could express those concepts simply using the language we normally speak and write in.

So if you have any difficulty in completing this activity, one way you could try is to ask yourself 'what does this mean, in practical terms?' My answer to punctual was 'arrive on time.' Where I used the word 'punctual' as the concept and the short phrase 'arrive on time' as firstly, what it means in practical terms and secondly, personalised to how I write and speak.

Okay, I'll let you go and complete these activities. When you are done, I'll see you in the next tutorial.

WB15 – Enhance Our Personal Attributes

Step 1.

Step 2. Rewrite your list of Personal Attributes (from WB08) so that they items relevant to the job you want to gain are listed from most important to least important (to employers)

Step 3. In the right hand column, complete activity WB15.

	(Attribute)	(Language)	
	e.g. punctual	arrive on time	

TUTORIAL 04. PERSONAL PROFILE Section

This is video 4 of 5 for Lesson: Personal Profile section.

Welcome back. This is Tutorial 04 of Lesson 05 the Personal Profile section in the Develop Your Content module of the Create a Functional Resume course.

In the previous tutorial, I sent you off to complete Student Workbook activity WB15, which is simultaneously our finalising our Core Skills section details and starting to develop our Personal Profile section details too.

So now that you have completed those three activities, we are now able to get closer to the next workbook activity, which is blending our now enhanced and personalised attributes into our skill statements.

Blend opportunities

To finish off our Core Skills details, we now need to look at the skill statements we wrote in WB13 and see if any of our new practical term expressions can be added to any of those statements.

When you find one – which you should be able to find appropriate places – write out the enhanced skill statement in the space provided at WB16.

Each time you find a skill statement that you can blend an attribute into, remember to tick the attribute off as addressed, and cross out the skill statement too, so you can see that this has been used. Because, like for our core skills, we only want to address each once, and because we are working in three different parts of our workbook, it could quite easily become confusing.

There are 4 steps to this activity. These are:

Step 1. Is to pick an attribute from WB15 – start with the most important and progressively work your way through to the least important.

Step 2. Is to examine your skill statements – and look for opportunities to comfortably blend the practical term somewhere into any of your skill statements. That could be at the beginning or in the middle of the skill statement.

IF you find a place to blend the attribute into a Skill statement, then complete Step 3.

If you find you can't blend the attribute into any of your skill statements, then complete Step 4 instead.

Step 3. If it does fit, write out the blended statement in WB16. Tick off the attribute at WB15 and cross off the skill statement at WB13.

Step 4. If the attribute doesn't fit with any of the skill statements you have at WB13, move on to the next attribute on your list.

Some people will find it easier to see the blend opportunities than others, not because they have better ability in doing so (that that will factor into it) but because some skill statements will lend themselves better than others. Don't worry if you can't blend all of your attributes.

While you work, just ask yourself 'How – and where – can I slip a person attribute into this skill statement so I avoid having to write personal attribute statements?'

Once you've completed the activity, hopefully you'll have a mix of:

- blended skill statements
- leftover skill statements, and
- leftover attributes.

Okay, I'll end this tutorial so that you can go and complete this activity. Once you are done, I'll meet you in the next tutorial.

WB16 – Blend Opportunities
Use this section to blend attributes into the skill statements written at WB13 in the last lesson. Once an attribute in the WB15 list has been used, use the last column to show that it has been dealt with.

Skill 1	
Action Word:	
Specifics:	
Result / Benefit:	

Skill 2	
Action Word:	

Specifics:	
Result / Benefit:	

Skill 3	
Action Word:	
Specifics:	
Result / Benefit:	

Skill 4	
Action Word:	
Specifics:	
Result / Benefit:	

Skill 5	
Action Word:	
Specifics:	
Result / Benefit:	

Skill 6	
Action Word:	
Specifics:	

Result / Benefit:	

Skill 7	
Action Word:	
Specifics:	
Result / Benefit:	

Skill 8	
Action Word:	
Specifics:	
Result / Benefit:	

Skill 9	
Action Word:	
Specifics:	
Result / Benefit:	

Skill 10	
Action Word:	
Specifics:	
Result / Benefit:	

WB17 – Transfer details to Master Worksheet

Once completed, you may now transfer these enhanced skill statements over to the Core Skills list in Functional Resume Master Worksheet. (not all of the skill statements will have had attributes added. Keeping the order of priority, transfer the skills statements and blended skill statements over to the Core Skills list in the functional resume master worksheet).

TUTORIAL 05. PERSONAL PROFILE Section

This is video 5 of 5 for Lesson: Personal Profile section.

Welcome back. This is Tutorial 05 of Lesson 05 the Personal Profile section in the Develop Your Content module of the Create a Functional Resume course.

In the previous tutorial, I sent you off to complete Student Workbook activity WB16 Blend Opportunities, which is our simultaneously finalising the Core Skills section details and the beginning of developing our Personal Profile section details too.

Now that you have blended as many attributes as you could into your skill statements, our next steps are to:

1. Transfer our Skill Statements across to the master worksheet,
2. Convert any remaining attributes we have left on our list into Personal Attribute statements, and then
3. Transfer your Personal Attribute statements across to the master worksheet.

Ideally, we don't want any more than 6 bullet points in this section.

Why six?

Because we want the employers focus to stay on believing we can do the job and do it well rather than have them probing too much into who we are as a person.

Think about when you meet someone new at a party. If the person goes on and on and on and on about themselves, we tend to end up disliking them and we mentally start tuning out and do our best to stifle our desire to yawn. When we first meet the person, we are generally interested enough to learn a little bit about who they are and are happy to tell them a little bit about who we are in return – but we disengage when the conversation becomes one-sided as they start going into their entire life story.

What about those of you who have Facebook and are a member of a Facebook group or few relating to your personal interests. How do you feel when someone new joins the group and the only posts they make to the group is to sell whatever product or service they want you to buy?

Even when you are possibly interested in the product or service, most people hold back – that is, they may ask for more information, but they generally don't proceed with the purchase until later, once a bit of relationship has been established.

Why?

Because in both situations the other person isn't building relationship, they are imparting awareness, that underneath meet only their own needs, or only for their gain. Put simply, they aren't balancing the interest and respect we have given them with an equal interest and respect for us in return. Therefore, they come across as too self-absorbed, too domineering, too salesy, which lowers their likeability.

We want to avoid demonstrating the negative sides to our nature like them, so that we don't destroy our likeability that we've built with the employer. So, like a cat burglar, we want to get in and out of the building quickly. Have you noticed that cat burglars plan their heists long before they commit their crime? They are not opportunists; they are careful and meticulous planners who cover every angle and contingency possible.

We could easily make ourselves look too self-absorbed in our written communications too, where the only message we seem to impart is 'I want you to know this, this, this, this and this about me. Oh and this, this, this, this and this.'

That's why I encourage you to address only the personal attributes the employers have told us they are looking for, rather than following the pact to start from us.

Now, if the Talk Learning Style is predominantly your learning style, then be aware that you will probably internally struggle against scaling back on how much to tell employers because your natural inclination will be to want to tell them as much as you possibly can. So Talk Learners, you will need to curtail that natural urge.

Okay, we've now covered everything you need to know and are ready to start on writing Personal Attribute statements.

Write personal attribute statements

Let's go over how to write a Personal Attribute statement, for those of you who need me to take you through the process.

Let's say you finished up the last activity blending attributes into your skill statements, and you still have the attribute of 'team player' on your list, and you've established that this attribute is highly important to the employer, and you fully understand and appreciate that you can't just write 'I am a strong team player.'

How can we convey this attribute?

Example

When I asked myself the question, 'what does this mean, in practical terms?' I came up with it means pitching in and helping colleagues.

From this, it prompts me to ask, 'how do you pitch in and help colleagues.'

And the initial response to that was, 'by helping them do their job during business periods, even though it is not my job.'

After this I asked the question, 'Can I be more specific' a few times, and edited my sentence so that I was happy with how it read the personal attribute statement I came up with looked like this:

- Pitched in to help colleagues during peak periods by serving clients and answering incoming calls, as well as sharing ideas during meetings and voluntarily keeping them informed of important updates following their absences.

Pitched in... sharing ideas... informing others of important updates. That is the work of a good team player, isn't it?

As you can see, I used the same formula that we used for Core Skills, which was:

Strong Active Verb + Specific Supportive Details + Results = Compelling Statement.

And I followed the five steps too. Only, this time, step one was 'Choose an Attribute' instead of the previous Choose a Skill.

As I was building up the statement, I asked 'Can I be more specific?' a few times, and because I had workplace examples that I could draw from, I used those examples. However, if you haven't worked previously you can draw upon non-workplace examples here too.

I reread my sentence to make sure I was happy with how it was worded, and asked the second question, 'Does this paint a clear mental picture?' once I was done – and edited my sentence until I felt that it read well and painted the picture I intended.

So, you have 3 workbook activities to complete to finish off this lesson.

1. Transfer your Skill Statements across to the master worksheet, and
2. Convert any remaining attributes we have left on our list into Personal Attribute statements, and then
3. Transfer your Personal Attribute statements across to the master worksheet.

When you are done, mark this lesson complete so that you can access the next lesson, which is Part C – Historical information sections.

And can I just say, you are on a role, and are fast approaching the finish line. Keep up your very great progress! Thank you for watching, see you in the next lesson.

Strong Active Verb + Specific Supportive Details + Results = Compelling Skill Statement

The 5 steps you need to follow are:

Step 1. Choose a Personal Attribute.
Step 2. Choose an appropriate Action Word
Step 3. Add Numbers and Quantifiable Amounts
Step 4. Add Results and Outcomes
Step 5. Ensure targeted, positive language is used

The question you need to ask yourself for each skill is: *Could I be more specific?*

And, once you have completed writing your sentence, ask: Does this sentence paint a strong mental picture about me and the situation?

WB18 – Transform Attributes into Personal Attribute Statements
Use this section to transform your remaining attributes into personal attribute statements

Attribute 1	
Action Word:	
Specifics:	
Result / Benefit:	

Attribute 2	
Action Word:	
Specifics:	
Result / Benefit:	

Attribute 3	
Action Word:	

Specifics:	
Result / Benefit:	

Attribute 4	
Action Word:	
Specifics:	
Result / Benefit:	

Attribute 5	
Action Word:	
Specifics:	
Result / Benefit:	

Attribute 6	
Action Word:	
Specifics:	
Result / Benefit:	

Attribute 7	
Action Word:	
Specifics:	

Result / Benefit:	

Attribute 8	
Action Word:	
Specifics:	
Result / Benefit:	

Attribute 9	
Action Word:	
Specifics:	
Result / Benefit:	

Attribute 10	
Action Word:	
Specifics:	
Result / Benefit:	

WB19 – Transfer details to Master Worksheet

Once completed, you may now transfer these enhanced skill statements over to the Personal Profile list in Functional Resume Master Worksheet.

BONUS TUTORIAL

Welcome back. This is a bonus tutorial added in response to student feedback.

We have been asked to explain WHY listing personal attributes in word or short phrase form makes them Unprovable (Or Disputable) Claims, so we've created this additional video to explain it.

I'll start by providing the dictionary meaning of the words:

- Claim
- Subjective, and
- Disputable

Claim

- Claim means to state or assert that something is the case, typically without providing evidence or proof.

Subjective

- Subjective means based on or influenced by personal feelings, tastes or opinions.

Disputable

- Disputable means not established as fact, and so is open to question or debate.

Unprovable (or Disputable) Claims

Whereas a hiring manager will be more inclined to believe what you tell (or, are claiming) your skills are; they will never be as inclined to believe you about what you claim are your personal attributes.

One, because every jobseeker seems to use those same seven or so attributes which we listed in the tutorial explaining what a typical Personal Profile section looks like; and two, because too many people who claim for example that they are reliable and punctual very quickly prove through their actions that they aren't reliable or punctual whatsoever.

Because personal attribute statements give the context they become more believable even though it is still just your word. It is the evidence to support why you are saying you have the attribute which makes them less disputable.

For example, I could just tell you 'I am a punctual person.' And because you don't know me, you don't have a way to know whether this true – or whether I am off the wall delusional. It is just me stating my own opinion about the attribute.

But, when I provide you with concrete supportive details to support my stating this about myself, such as I generally arrive early to appointments because I like having time to find parking, and I love to use the wait time to read a book that I take with me or to write ideas into my notebook that I carry in my handbag when I am working on a writing project, it is these supportive details that lead you to being more inclined to believe that I am speaking the truth.

And you'll be inclined to believe me because I'm not claiming or suggesting that I am never ever late. The words 'I like to...' leave just enough room in your mind and my own that I could run late one time without ruining my integrity, because one-off lateness is a possibility for everyone.

You, like a hiring manager, would take my punctuality on faith. You will still be able to determine my punctuality for yourself in the future – from your own observation, or by speaking to an independent person. But for now, you'll just accept my word for it.

But if I foolishly said to you, 'I am a punctual person. I always arrive on time,' straightaway your logical brain would start challenging all the reasons why I could never always arrive on time – I could get stuck in traffic or break down (if I'm driving); I could write down the wrong appointment time...

What other things is your logical brain telling you could make me a liar about always being punctual?

And lastly, even if I am accurate or completely delusional, my stating I am punctual is just my own personal opinion. You could eventually reach the same conclusion, or the opposite; but I'll always consider myself punctual – and therefore I'm just being subjective.

So, I hope that adequately answers the question of why personal attributes can be unprovable (and disputable) claims.

Thanks for watching.

LESSON 06.

TRAINING, EDUCATION, QUALIFICATIONS AND LICENSING SECTION(S)

LESSON INTRO

Thanks for joining me again.

You are now up to Lesson 06 Training, Education, Qualification and Licensing section in the Develop Your Resume Content module of the Write a Functional Resume course.

This lesson is the first Historical Information component that we include in our Functional resume. The other Historical Information component is our Work History which we will cover in the next lesson.

You probably already know exactly what this section addresses, and although you might also have a strong idea of how to address this section in your resume, I want to make sure you get it right, so I will cover everything for those that don't.

What we will cover are the same 5 aspects that we have covered for each of the previous sections. These are:

1. What the section is
2. What the section looks like
3. What alternatives – if any – you can use,
4. How to decide on specifics to include in this section, and
5. How to write those details so that they are likely to be interesting to a Hiring Manager.

So, when you are ready, head on over and join me in the first tutorial.

TUTORIAL 01. TRAINING, EDUCATION, QUALIFICATIONS & LICENSING Section

This is video 1 of 2 for Lesson: Training, Education, Qualifications & Licensing section.

Welcome to Tutorial 01 of Lesson 6 Training, Education, Qualifications and Licensing section in the Development Your Resume Content module of the Write a Functional Resume course.

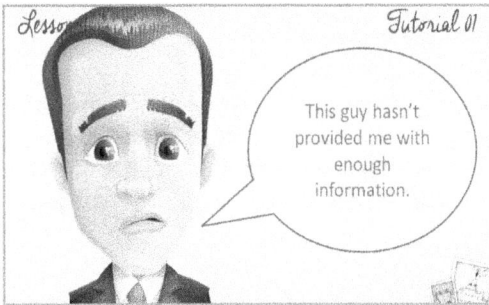

You may be surprised by just how many jobseekers who are applying for, say, a Forklift Driver role, don't specify anywhere on their resume that they have a current Forklift Licence. The jobseeker expects the hiring manager to work this out from their history in doing this line of work as their career.

Equally, you may be surprised by how many older workers, let's say those who are 45 years of age or older, who left school at least 25 years previously who include details of their high school education in their resume.

In other words, we have jobseekers who are either not providing enough information to show their suitability for the role (like in that first example) or are providing too much detail in their applications (like those in that second example).

We already know and appreciate that it is important to get this type of thing right, so this lesson will be about learning what that balance is for our educational and training type details.

What is the Training, Education, Qualifications and Licensing section?

This section is more than just what our formal education is or was.

This resume section recognises that learning and qualifications for a job can be gained from outside of just school and formal education; it recognises that some of what we have learned through other types of training may be fully relevant to the type of work we are seeking to gain; and therefore is fully appropriate to include in our resume.

Most of us went to school and completed the compulsory years. Some of you then left high school and got your first job, others continued on to complete additional school years and perhaps also went on to do a formal course of study at university, college or trade school. Some of you have completed training as part of your professional development in the jobs you've held, others have self-studied topics you have interest in which could help you in your work; yet others haven't done any study or training since leaving school – because you couldn't get out of there fast enough.

Did you learn how to drive when you reached the age that entitled you to do so? Why did you learn to drive? Was it because you wanted the personal freedom to drive yourselves from A to B in your own or your parent's car? Or was it because you needed it to get the type of job you wanted?

Regardless of what lead you to gaining your driver's licence or how long ago that was, many of you may now use this skill in a small or big way in relation to your jobs whether you thought you would need it for work purposes or not..

In almost every industry there are jobs that require the person to be the holder of a specific licence, permit, registration, ticket, card, check, or certificate of some kind or to have completed a specific training course – either before they can gain that type of work, or must be successfully completed within a specific timeframe following commencing in the job.

Most certificates, licences, tickets, permits, cards, checks and the like are issued by a statutory authority, as a result of the person completing the training and standardised testing, which once successfully passed demonstrates that their competency is at or above the minimum standard determined by industry.

It is these requirements, or qualifications, relevant to the type of work we seek to gain and are often the things that make you qualified to do the work, which belong in this resume section.

Oh, and to make it easier for you and I, throughout the rest of this lesson, I'll just refer to that long list of certificates, licences, tickets, permits, etc as either 'requirements' or 'qualifications' when I can, so please keep that in mind as we progress.

What the section looks like.

The section is another bullet listing (that is either with or without the actual bullets dots depending on your personal style preference.)

The key part here is because we are creating a Functional format resume, we only need to include details of the specific qualifications relating to the job or that will give us a competitive edge in the job (not just our application), so that the hiring manager can see that you have the necessary qualifications:

1. To be eligible to apply,
2. That you can do the job,
3. and will view you as being able to do it well,

...without being too specific on all the finer details which could lead to age discrimination, identity theft or 'not for us' decisions.

Any skills, capabilities or even personal attributes that we have developed as a result of our qualifications should be listed within our Core Skills and Personal Profile sections, because those are the two appropriate sections to 'sell' our ability, suitability and fit. Our Training, Education, Qualification and Licensing section is just a place for us to show our eligibility and to anchor where those skills and attributes we have claimed we have were developed from and to support our being ready to step into the role.

What alternatives – if any – can you use?

Now, because we have chosen the functional format and we only need to provide the barest of details to support what we have written in our Core Skills and Personal Profile sections, we can simply group all of our relevant specifics into the one listing if necessary – which is why I entitled this lesson Training, Education, Qualification and Licensing, because it covers the whole gamut of qualification-based requirements.

But, if we have a lot of ground to cover – that is, you have a wide range of certificates, licences, tickets, permits, cards and checks etc – then you may want or need to separate out those details into specific categories, if you wish. So that no single section becomes over-filled with details which can make the section lengthy and difficult to read.

For those of you with only a few details to add to this section, you are better off grouping them into the one listing so that they are presented in a logical fashion.

And I would encourage you though to avoid titling your section as 'Education' or 'Educational History', as those two titles restricts the information you can include down to just formal qualifications and certificates.

Instead, I recommend using a title that allows for broader inclusion of details, like 'Qualifications & Licensing' or similar, as it opens the range of qualifications we can address for the employer's benefit. Plus, by eliminating the word history from the title, even though we are dealing with historical based facts, we are making the section show a level of professional currency to the specifics, rather than implying an outdated-ness of them – which is a good thing.

It is these types of little things that can have the greatest impact on how the hiring manager views us as favourable or unfavourable.

How to decide on specifics to include in this section.

As we have done in each of our past lessons, we are going to use the information we gained from our Job Advertisement side activity to help us develop the content for this section as our starting point for deciding what qualifications we must address.

And everything else we have done is just something we need to decide whether it is relevant to our specific job and therefore appropriate to include, or doesn't relate to the job or is outdated and therefore is unnecessary details – which can lower the effectiveness of our resume if we include it.

Every other personal attribute that we believe we have, but which the employers haven't specified as being important to them, we will need to decide whether it is relevant to our job type and therefore appropriate to include, or doesn't related to the job and therefore should be left out.

But before we race over to our workbook, I want to discuss a few rules and best practices we should consider for this section.

The first is to only include 4 to 5 items in our Qualifications & Licensing list.

The main reason we don't want to list any more than five (5) items in our Qualifications & Licensing section is so that the information complements the dominant sections of our resume instead of overpowering them.

By this stage in the Hiring Manager's review of our application, they have seen our skills to have already decided you may be suitable, and then they were curious enough to try-you-on-for-size so took mental note of your attributes. If we still have their attention the rest of our details just reinforces what they already have learned about us, and anchors the where, when and in what situation you developed those skills. In other words, we showed them our skills in action, and now we are telling them where that action took place – which is our Educational or Work-related history.

Assuming they have decided you are still in contention for the position from what they have viewed so far, they are now on the verge of making a decision – to place your application on their yes or maybe pile. So we don't want to bog them down with too many details.

Short and sweet is best. So they don't change their mind to put your application in their no pile.

Therefore, we want to give them a nice simple listing of our relevant qualifications and licensing, and then – and this is the hardest part for most jobseekers to embrace – let them ask us over the phone or during an interview about anything else they would like further information on.

Too many bullet points in a listing are a reading turn off for most people.

So, if you think you might end up with more than 5 items on your list, you will need to either cut your listing down, or divide your specifics into two groups or categories

1. Qualifications, and
2. Licensing.

That is, create two smaller listings instead of one larger listing.

Resume length

The next best practice we need to consider is that we need to keep our resume to an acceptable 1 or 2 page final length.

The functional resume format looks best visually when it is exactly one page or two pages in length. And this section is one of the places where you can add to or cut down on to get your content up or down in size.

So, if you are on track to create a one-page, you need to address only the most important qualification and licensing details so that the hiring manager can see you have what they are asking for, or you risk extending your resume content to fall onto a second page by only a line or few – which can look stupid.

Limit details to last ten year period

The next best practice is that we need to keep our details to the last ten year period.

Back in the Foundations section of this course, I briefly discussed that we should keep our resume to the past 5 to 10 years because anything over that is either outdated or at a basic level which we (should) have grown on from since then.

Employers want to hire people who possess current skills in the type of job, and generally they will dismiss outdated ones as unimportant and outdated if you go beyond the 10 year maximum. So just because you did a course, doesn't mean you should automatically include it.

In all likelihood, courses that you took more than 5 years ago, have probably been updated or even replace since you did it, to keep them in line with modern practices and current industry expectations.

The next best practice to consider is what part of the qualification we tell the employer and what we can leave out.

For courses

The specifics that you need to include for courses are:

- the title of your qualification – because every qualification has a proper title (even if you personally don't know what that title is), you should use it, because there is a strong chance that the employer will know it, and not using the right title just lowers the quality of your resume

- courses you have fully completed, or are near completion and you have full confidence that you will successfully qualify to gain certification, and
- the pass level – only if the subject is graded and you pass at a Distinction or High Distinction level, because when you are a high achiever in something you should let employers know this as it could give you a competitive edge over lesser qualified applicants.

You can leave out:

- **Courses you did not complete** – as in you enrolled but dropped out for whatever reason, because negative value judgements can be drawn from this and we don't want to reduce how employers view us,
- **Attainment dates, institute completed through and institute location** – because these are extra details that don't provide any value to the employer but which can increase your risk of having your identity stolen
- **The modules undertaken** – because the impressive part is your completing the course, and employers are generally aware of what modules are included in the nationally recognised courses, and
- **The pass level, if you pass a graded subject only at Pass or Credit level** – because you have attained an average result and our resume is about making our self stand out and impress decision makers not show them we fit in with the majority.

And, because it is fully relevant to this section too, remember to avoid including:

- Age revealing specifics (direct or indirect)
- Specifics that are irrelevant to the job you are apply for, and
- Making the focus on your educational achievement instead of your capability to the job role and do it well.

For Licences, Permits etc

The specifics that you need to include for licences and permits etc are:

- Use the proper licence title. If industry calls it a Driver's Licence C Class, then you should list it as Driver's Licence C Class.

You should leave out:

- **The attainment or expiry dates** – because you are listing current qualifications, and these specifics are the extras that can lead to increased risk of having your identity stolen. If the employer needs to know these things, let them ask you for them during the job interview (they usually want to photocopy them to keep them on your employee record).

- Don't include *expired qualifications*

When I was an employment consultant I had one client who had been unemployed for over 2 years who became upset while I updated his resume to remove the many expired licences and permits from his listings.

'No, no, no, no,' he said, quite upset. 'Leave those in; they prove I used to have what they need.'

This jobseeker was a notoriously difficult man to work with, and when I tried to tackle the issue nicely he immediately dismissed every bit of advice being given – by me and other consultants.

Finally I asked in frustration, 'Exactly how does proving what licences and permits you used to but no longer have help you get the job when all employers care about is finding staff with current ones? What benefit or advantage does keeping them in give you, because all I can see is how it ruins your employability?'

He was unable to answer those questions. His only remaining protest was that by cutting those out it would make his resume shorter. And when I replied 'that's the whole point of my revising your resume' he struggled again, but once I had finished cutting his resume down from 3.5 pages to just 2 he was happy because he could see that he looked more suitable for the type of work he sought, not less which is what he was actually concerned would happen.

I didn't get to explain my reasons to him, but I will do this for you. The reason I cut out those expired licences and permits is because they didn't do anything to contribute towards making a good impression; they were actually doing the opposite, creating a poor one. When I first saw them, I shook my head and wondered 'Why has he got these in here?' And that is exactly the negative question most hiring managers would ask when they saw them.

Okay, we've now covered what the section is, what the section looks like, the alternatives, and how to decide upon the details to include and don't include in this section. In the next tutorial, we will start doing some workbook activities again, so we can complete the final step which is writing those details so that they are likely to be interesting to the hiring manager.

Thank you for watching, I'll meet you in the next tutorial.

TUTORIAL 02. TRAINING, EDUCATION, QUALIFICATIONS & LICENSING Section

This is video 2 of 2 for Lesson: Training, Education, Qualifications & Licensing section.

Welcome back. This is Tutorial 02 of Lesson 6 the Training, Education, Qualifications and Licensing section in the Development Your Resume Content module of the Write a Functional Resume course.

In the last tutorial we looked at what the section is, what it looks like, the alternatives to this section, and how to decide upon the details to include and not include within the section.

We will now cover capturing and writing those details so that they are likely to be interesting to a hiring manager.

There will be a few workbook activities in this tutorial, and you will need to pause the video in order to complete the activity.

Let's begin, shall we?

5. How to write those details so that they are likely to be interesting to a Hiring Manager.

Step 1.

We will start by doing a workbook activity. In a moment I will get you to pause this video and in the space provided at WB20, write down a list of all the licences, permits, checks, that you have and the training courses you have completed.

Step 2.

When you have done this, I want you to compare the list of qualifications and requirements that the employer is looking for, which we wrote down in WB11, and place a tick in the space provided at WB20 for each requirement where you are a job match – that is the employer is looking for it and you have it.

These entries will become the most important training, education, qualification and licensing details that you must mention in your resume.

Okay, you can PAUSE this video now to complete those 2 activities.

WB20 – My Portfolio of Qualifications

Licences, Permits, Checks, Cards, Tickets etc

Type	Title	
e.g. Licence	e.g. NSW Driver's Licence C Class	

Training & Educational Certificates

Enrollee or	Title	
Graduate	e.g. Certificate III in Business Administration	

Welcome back.

Now for whatever reason, not all of you will have all the qualifications requirements that employers are looking for. If this is you, then you will need to consider the impact this may have upon your applications – will it make you a less appealing candidate compared to those that do posses those requirements now, will it slow your success down, what actions can you take to minimise the impact on your jobsearch success, that type of thing.

If you can, it may assist your cause if while you are looking for work you also work towards closing your employment gaps. In other words, try not to 'park' yourself into an activity, if you can avoid it. Jobseekers who continue to look for work while addressing their gaps generally find work quicker than those that stop jobsearching while they do a course or undertake work experience etc.

At the very least you should consider ways and means of working around it the best way you can, and be prepared to discuss this aspect and your ways to work around it with an employer during an interview when you gain one.

Our next thing to look at is what qualifications do you have but employers haven't stated are required?

First of all we have to ask, 'Is their list complete?'

Again, this will require us to think carefully about the job and compare what we have written at WB11 with what we know and think employers need too.

For example, maybe an office worker has completed a touch typing course, and employers haven't stated this as a necessity, but you realise that this would give you an advantage in the role – because touch typing raises your efficiency level by something like 45% (or the study I read a long time ago cited that percentage), so including details of your per minute or keystrokes per hour may give you a competitive edge over applicant that are hung and peck typists.

Now, it's not necessarily that the employers list is incomplete, that detail might just be a 'nice to have' or a 'good to let them know' that gives you an advantage. Either way, because it is relevant to the job type, it belongs in your resume – after their stated most important details.

So our next two (2) activities are to:

1.   Look over the employers list (WB11) and determine its completeness. Is there any important qualification –related detail missing? Add it.

And,

2. Then look over your qualification history and determine which of the things you have listed is relevant to the type of work you seek. Is there anything in your list that could boost your potential suitability in the hiring managers' view? Is there anything that could give you a competitive edge over other applicants? Tick them; we will include these in your resume.

Okay, you can PAUSE this video now to complete those 2 activities.

Welcome back.

Do you have any qualification history left on your personal list that you have not ticked as what employers are looking for or will boost your suitability? Then these are specifics that do not belong in your resume.

So that leaves us with two last steps to complete:

1. Rank our details from most important to least important, and then
2. Transfer our entries to the master resume worksheet.

Rank our details from most important to least important.

Again, we want to present our details so that hiring managers see the items that are most important to them first – to get them making mental ticks of compatibility and suitability. Every item that is on your WB11 list is more important than your 'good to let them knows'.

Once we have numbered our listing in the order that we should present them, you can then transfer your Training, Education, Qualifications and Licensing section details over to the Functional Resume Master Worksheet. The Master Worksheet has 2 sections for you, but you don't have to use both if you only have 5 or less items to list.

So, I'll let you go and complete these last two activities, and when you are done, I'll see you in the next lesson.

Thank you for watching.

WB21 – Transfer details to Master Worksheet
Once completed, you may now transfer these enhanced skill statements over to the Qualifications & Requirements list in Functional Resume Master Worksheet.

LESSON 07.

WORK HISTORY & SKILL ACQUIREMENT SECTION

LESSON 07. WORK HISTORY & SKILL ACQUIREMENT Section

In this lesson, what we will look at is slightly different to our previous sections.

We will cover:

1. What the Employment section is and if it is required
2. The 3 specifics to include
3. How to list them, and
4. Key considerations and best practices for creating this section
5. Specifics that are not necessary relating to our work history

TUTORIAL 01. WORK HISTORY & SKILL ACQUIREMENT Section

This is video 1 of 2 for Lesson: Work History & Skill Acquirement section.

This is Tutorial 01 of Lesson 7 Employment and Skill Acquirement section in the Development Your Resume Content module of the Write a Functional Resume course.

In the Structure lesson back near the beginning of the course, we learned that the key difference between the functional resume and the other two formats lies in how the core skills are separated away – or divorced – from the employment or other circumstance from where the skills were gained, or tasks performed.

Seeing as we created our Core Skills section already and the two sections are needed to make up to the whole all that is left here is to provide the remaining information of where we gained the skills we listed in that core skills section.

And that should be relatively easy, because all you really need to do is add just three key specifics into a listing. Those specifics are:

- A position Title, the
- Company name, and a
- timeframe for the position

But before we dive in to completing this section in our workbook, I have a few key considerations and best practices for creating this section that I want to discuss.

So let's go through them.

Not just paid employment

Most people just think of this section as being a place to list each of their previous paid positions held. But when we were creating our core skills section content, I encouraged you to consider more than just your previous paid positions. Specifically, I encouraged you to consider the skills you gained from within formal work situations, such as employment, self employment and agency work, and also from within informal work situations, such as voluntary work, work experience, community participation and even personal situations.

It doesn't matter whether you developed in the skills in a full time, part time, casual capacity; on a permanent or temporary basis, with contracts that were fixed terms or open ended and ongoing; the key point here is if you developed a relevant skill to have listed it in your core skills section, then you now need to create a 'work history' type section to provide the remaining skill development details so that your resume paints a

Core Skill gained from previous paid job (employment)	• Position Title • Company Name • Date range (or Accumulative Total)
Core Skill gained from unpaid work (voluntary work, work experience, community / social participation)	• Position Title • Company Name • Date range (or Accumulative Total)

fuller picture about those skills listed.

Titling your 'Work History' section

The next consideration is in the titling of this section.

Naming your section goes hand in hand with the actual specifics you will include in this section. For example, if you are only going to list your work history specifics, you could indeed just title your section as either Work or Employment; whereas if you are going to include specifics from skill development, then you don't want to mislead employers by entitling the section as just Employment.

Your Personal Circumstance

So, your personal background will have a strong bearing here on how you handle this simple section, so you will need to exercise your discretion about what will work best for you.

For example, if you have worked in the same or a closely similar role in the past to what you are going to be applying to in the future, then the path for you is rather straightforward. Because each of your core skills listed in the core skills section was developed directly from your work history, you could simply entitle this section as Employment and then list each of your prior positions held, listing the position title, the company you worked for and the timeframe details of when you worked there – using either the Month and Year format or an Amount of Experience format, which I will discuss later in this lesson.

But, if you haven't worked in the same or a similar role to what you are going to be applying to, then the path isn't quite as straightforward, because it contains a few 'if this then do this' type scenarios.

What if you have worked previously, but those jobs were different to the job role that you will be applying to? Well, then your core skills section specifics are probably a mixture of transferrable workplace skills, gained within your past roles, as well as informal skill development, gain within your personal or workplace-like activities..

So, if you have, say, 5 core skills listed and you developed them in 5 different formal and informal places within your past, then you would need to 'anchor' them by listing those very 5 places in this section, so that your details are complete.

But, and you probably see the problem just as much as I see here.

Naming this section as employment doesn't quite work for you, does it – because it limits you to including only your previous employment details, and it leaves the rest of your core skills unanchored to where they were gained or making their inclusion jarring r misleading for the reader.

So, the way to be able to list non-workplace like circumstances and not have them jar or mislead is to get a bit more creative with this sections title – so that the section title is more encompassing and supportive to your broader skill development areas.

I suggest something like:

- Work & Skill Development, or
- Employment & Participation

... As your title, because those alternative title options enable you to list all of your core work skills experience regardless whether they were gain during voluntary work, community participation and even relevant personal situations – which is what we are aiming for.

Okay, so what if you have never worked previously, either at all or those of you who are returning after a significant employment break – I'm talking years out of the paid workforce here, rather than just months? Well, the same sort of alternatives will apply to you too.

Instead of titling your section 'work & skill development' or 'employment & participation', you could drop the words 'work' and 'employment' to just entitle the section something like, 'skill development', 'participation', 'related experience' or 'organisational highlights' – that sort of thing.

As I said, you may need to get creative in order to title your section so that it adequately encompasses the details you will be including within it. But on a visual level, the hiring manager will pick up that all the essential resume components are present.

Avoid the word History

Now, notice that in each of the previous example section titles, I have deliberately avoided using the word 'History' in any of them. This is because the word 'history' immediately implies a negative aspect of outdated-ness to the specifics.

Of course those details occurred naturally in the past, but that doesn't mean we should emphasis this fact. It may be only subtle, but dropping the word 'history' can help hiring managers to see your skills as professionally current – which is important if you have been out of work for more than 3 months, where your professional currency and therefore employment-likeability starts dropping at alarming speed.

Ten year history

Now, speaking of professional currency, I've said it earlier in this course and it is worth re-mentioning right now: resumes are not meant to lay down your entire life history; they are a document that profiles your relevant skills, experiences and capabilities for the type of work you seek to gain. Therefore, it is imperative that the details you provide demonstrate your professional currency – not just your capability and suitability to make you likeable – so I want to caution you about the time period of the details you include.

In the recruitment – or hiring – world, any skill, qualification or experience that is over ten years old is immediately viewed as being so far outdated it will have been superseded; and therefore is unlikely to generate employer interest, which makes including such older details futile.

Sure, you can have situations like once you have learned how to ride a bicycle you never forget how to do so; but for those who do get back on a bike, say, twenty years later, there is always an aspect of the person needing to conscious competence-ly re-learn how to ride again with confidence. Most people resuming old skills usually start off quite shakily and need time to build up to the unconscious competence shakiness-free level again.

When we look at things from the hiring perspective, employers generally seek to employ people who are unconsciously competent, that is, they are completely confident with their skills and experiences to be able to cope with and effectively handle any problem they encounter, and so employers are likely to dismiss or give lower consideration towards those whose skills and experience occurred anywhere between five to ten years or more years ago, because they know the person will need to go through that relearning build up period.

And, when faced with candidates who have professional currency, it can start to reduce your chance of their holding on to the likeability you have worked so hard to create within your application, especially if they need someone who is unconsciously competent in the skill now.

We want to hold on to hiring managers' favourable interest in us in every way we can. So, best practice is to keep our section specifics to within the last ten year period so that we don't trigger any potential negativity or disinterest in the hiring manager.

Remember, most industries are in an employer market, and it is already going to be more than competitive enough for us to get an in, without making things more difficult for ourselves.

So, whatever year you are currently in, just minus ten years, and everything that occurred before that can be left out unless you have an absolute solid and reasonable excuse to include it.

And of course, by keeping your details to the last ten year period, coincidentally, you also guard against revealing some specifics that could lead to discriminating against you based on age.

Okay, so we've covered the essential considerations, in the next tutorial, we will look at those three specific for a functional resume 'work history' section that we include a bit closer.

So, thank you for watching, and I'll see you in Tutorial 02.

TUTORIAL 02. WORK HISTORY & SKILL ACQUIREMENT Section

This is video 2 of 2 for Lesson: Work History & Skill Acquirement section.

This is Tutorial 2 of Lesson 7 Employment and Skill Acquirement section in the Development Your Resume Content module of the Write a Functional Resume course.

Welcome back. In Tutorial 01, we covered a few important considerations and best practices relating to the information intended for this 'work history' section.

Now, we will cover the three specific details that we include in this section for a functional resume.

Those 3 key specifics were:

- A position Title, the
- Company name, and a
- timeframe for the position / experience

We'll now go through each of those key specifics in turn.

Position Title

Most people have no problem knowing what the position titles were for their past paid employment roles, but it isn't always so straightforward when it comes to their self-employment, voluntary work, community participation and personal circumstances.

So, if you don't know what your position title was, or even if you didn't have one, the quick, easy and obvious solution is to just give yourself a relevant title that will adequately convey what you did, and will support what job you are aiming to gain.

Now let's look how that works in practicality.

If you are applying for, say, Office Admin work and you did touch typing, word processing, document creating etc for a local community group you are involved in, then it is perfectly acceptable to create a listing where you give yourself the position title of Typist, Admin Assistant, Office Administrator or even Document Creator if you wanted to – or whatever other title you deem suitably relevant to cover the role you performed or tasks you completed.

Now, continuing on with that Office Admin example, let's say you have never held a paid job in Office Admin work previously but you have done this in a couple of different informal work situations. In this scenario, it could really enhance the hiring manager viewing your potential suitability if you didn't list the exact same position title for each of your different circumstances. By varying your self-created titles slightly, you could possibly showcase more of your skill range, and thus better show your potential suitability.

The next point about Position Titles I would like to make is that you don't have to use the position title that a previous company you worked for gave you. I mean, that is just one employer's view of what the position is called, isn't it?

Sometimes, changing the position title for a previous position held will enable the hiring manager reviewing applications to see your skills more clearly, and or stop them being confused or mislead.

For example, I once had a client who had listed his job title as 'Product Distributor'. I'd never heard of this job title before, and because he hadn't written down what his duties had been, myself and co-workers speculated that he must have been involved in Sales-natured roles in the past, and was now trying to change career direction into roles for which he had no direct experience. With no obvious match in skills and experiences for the jobs he was applying to, we felt this jobseeker was going to have a tough time getting interviews, so this was a barrier we felt needed urgent addressing.

When I inevitably met the jobseeker client, he clarified that the Product Distributor position title was just the employers way of saying he had been a Forklift Driver. And suddenly, this clarification made it clear why he was applying to Warehouse Supervisor roles on his jobsearch record sheets.

I fixed up his resume and changed his position title from Product Distributor to Forklift Driver, so that in future applications the hiring managers could understand his employment history to see he did indeed have the very skills and experiences they were seeking, which instantly boosted his likeability and application success rate.

So, if the position title that you held could be confusing or misleading to the hiring manager like that, then please, you have my permissions to change your position title to something more aligned to your career direction, rather than let something like that stop you progressing.

That gentleman had had for a while suspected that employers were misinterpreting his skills, and that was the reason he wasn't getting success with finding a new job. But, he had kept that misleading position title because that's what the past employer had called the role and he wasn't aware that he was free to change it to something that would reflect more accurately what he had done. He was hesitate and felt guilty about my changing his position title until he got his first invite to attend an interview – after that he stopped worrying about having broken some unspoken rule that made his feel he had to stick to what the past employer had entitled it.

Company name

The next specific detail we need to include is the ***company name.***

Okay, this should be fairly straight forward too. Whichever company you worked for, volunteered at or completed work experience or community service with, is what you list in this section – after the position title.

When it comes to the finer details, it is more the position you held that can indicate the skills, experiences and capabilities you may have than knowing who you worked for.

For example, having a former position title of say, Typist, tells me what you did, and gives me a strong idea about what duties and responsibilities you may have held. In other words, I can make value judgements about what your skills, experiences, qualifications and capabilities are just by reading the position title alone.

Now, I don't know why, but for some reason a lot of resumes I have reviewed treat the employer name as being more important than the position, and I think this is a big mistake.

When I was reviewing applications for the various vacancies, I didn't care if the applicant previously worked at Theo's Cafe, Hayley's Bistro or Kookies Coffee Shop, the information I found more interesting, the detail I learn more about the applicant, was whether the position they held was as the waitress, the chef, the dishwasher, or even the owner / manager. Because that showed me more about how much of a match they were to the vacancy we had than what a company name ever will.

So unless you work in an industry where the employer name will be the most impressive detail, say you are a solicitor and once worked for the prestigious ABC Firm which sets the bar for high standards or results and is therefore highly regarded within the industry and would lead you to advancing in your career just from that company's prestige, it is best to make the previous roles you've held as your key detail for the section and just leave the company name to rightfully act as the supplementing component.

Now, it is important to note here that the company name is still needed though, because it resolves the mystery of where you gained your skills and experience.

Actually, if you are applying to jobs advertised by recruitment agencies, the company name detail is likely to help them work out if they should put your application forward to an employer. Maybe you have previously worked for the company they are hiring for, or the person they are dealing with used to work at one of your old employers? These unknown to you aspects could end up giving you an advantage, or equally be the cause of you not being considered – which is why you should strive to always leave on good terms with every employer, if you can.

Timeframe for the position / experience

The last specific detail to cover in this section is how much experience you have, expressed in length of time terms.

There are 2 ways you could handle this, and these are:

1. By listing the commencement and conclusion date range of your employment or involvement (which answers the question how long have you performed in that position), or
2. By providing an accumulative total – specified in months or years – for how much accumulated experience you have for a specific skill or task, from all sources (which answers the question how long have you been doing that?)

Hiring Managers prefer the length of experience when it is expressed as a date ranges because these show them exactly from when to when you worked in the job (or participated in the skill development); and they can become rather suspicious about applicants having something to hide if they don't include this information, or use the accumulative total alternative.

With the Date Range option, the way to list the specifics is by using the Month and Year (only) for both the start and finish timeframe. That is, you do not need the day of the month that you started, just the month and the year.

For example

January 2013 to June 2015 rather than 18th January 2013 to 23 June 2015.

You are free to choose variations like Jan 13 to Jun 15, or Jan 2013 to Jun 2015, if you like – as these are personal style preferences.

If you are still working in a particular job role or participating in your informal workplace-like situations, then you substitute the finish dates with either of the words 'Present' or 'Current' to indicate your still being in the role.

It is important to consider here that using the date range method often reveals employment gaps that could become problematic for jobseekers, because if hiring managers are interested in your as a potential candidate they will want to know why there is an employment gap and if you reach the job interview stage, will want such gaps explained to them, so they can work out whether there is a potential problem for them or increased risk in hiring you, or not.

It is okay to tell employers that that one month employment gap was while you were looking for work because your contract ended, or that a longer gap was because you were made redundant or took a career break to raise your family or care for another person. The employment gaps that will be of concern to hiring managers are reasons like being fired or otherwise had your employment terminated for bad attitude, behavioural or performance issues.

One of the 'tricks' many jobseekers employ is to leave out their employment dates in the

hope of disguising problems within their past; but it is oftentimes their omission of such details that sends up the red flag warning to experienced hiring managers, who are well versed in what tricks jobseekers employ for various reasons. So, follow good rules and implement good strategies, but don't resort to cheap tricks which can backfire on the applicant.

The alternative method of showing you have experience for the type of work or time in a particular position, though it is not as effective as the date range, is to provide an accumulative total of your experience, such as 18 months experience, 3 years experience etc.

This method is great for disguising job hopping and employment gaps, but be aware that hiring managers will remain somewhat wary of candidates who use this method, as they will wonder what the person is trying to hide that led them to not using the date range. On the plus side, though, not all jobseekers who use this method are trying to hide something, they could just be helpfully summarising how much experience they have in this line of work, so it would be better to use this method than to not provide any of this third detail whatsoever.

Information that should not be included.

One of the most appealing aspects of the functional resume is its simplicity; so care needs to be taken to not over-complicating things.

Pay rates

On a holistic level, there is so much more details we could tell employers about our paid and unpaid workplace skills and their acquirement; but the key here is that those details are additional specifics, that are simply unnecessary either at all or during the application stage. Actually, you could very well harm your application if you were to include some of those extras.

For example, part of paid employment means getting paid, so it would be easy to think we should state what our annual or hourly rate was. But, there is a time and place for such discussions, and the application stage is not it. Those discussions come later, during the interview or job offer stages, and to raise the issue prematurely will be very off-putting for employers.

As a general rule, wait for an employer to raise such issues. The employer is the one with the vacancy, so let them lead or be in control of what happens and when. To do the opposite, can just make you seem uncooperative or difficult to work with.

I know you want to make sure you will be paid an amount you want to be paid, and you don't want to waste time on pursuing jobs that don't meet your financial expectations, so if you really want to know this upfront check the job listing to see if they have indicated the pay rate, research the company to gain insight or do a Pay or Award check to see what the minimum rates are. The point here is to wait for the employer to express high interest in you as a potential candidate before you have a money related discussion with them, or you could un-impress them to such an extent they end your candidacy with them.

Job Basis and Capacity

Another specific that is unnecessary is the basis to which you worked or were involved. That is, whether you did so on a full time, part time or casual basis, in a permanent or temporary capacity.

Most hiring managers will make an assumption that fits in with standard industry practice for basis and capacity.

For example, the fast food industry employing teenagers generally offer employment on a part time or casual basis, and employees must be rostered (and or work) a certain amount of hours per week as a legal minimum. Any hours worked over that are bonus for the employee. So future employers will assume you worked part time or casual with a minimum of roughly 10 hours per week.

It could be detrimental to your application if you specify that you only worked part time or casually in a role in circumstances where the employer may assume full time hours are involved. If they want to be certain that your 1 years worth of experience is from full time employment, please let them ask you that during a job interview rather than providing the answer in your application – which is you introducing issues to be addressed into your application.

We are not encouraging you to lie in your applications; we are simply saying not to volunteer information that could cause the hiring manager to determine you are not right for them. ALWAYS answer their questions honestly, but make it something they ask you about.

And lastly, because we are creating a functional resume and have already written our core skills section content, there is no need to include any further skill statements or otherwise introduce any further information about the duties and responsibilities you previously held. If you have outstanding information like this maybe you need to go back and revisit your core skills section, or check out Lesson 08. Other (Possibly Relevant) Sections.

So, with everything I can think of regarding the work history section now covered, it is time for us to turn to our Student Workbook again to complete this lesson's activity.

WORKBOOK ACTIVITY

You will notice in the work history section of the student workbook, at activity WB22, there is space for you to develop a portfolio of your formal and informal work history.

But, because we don't need to prepare the information we will include in the section like we did in previous lessons, if you want, you can leave that for another time and just go straight to the Functional Resume Master Worksheet at the back of the workbook to add your details directly into the Master Worksheet.

Reverse Chronological Order

Oh, and just because you have chosen the functional resume format, doesn't mean you get to escape listing your work history section details in reverse chronological order. That is the standard best practice for all resume types.

So, when listing your details, start with the most current 'role' and each subsequent line thereafter travels back in time until your last line is the first time you did something – keeping it all to within the last ten year period, of course (unless you have very good reason to break this rule).

Okay, that's all we need to know and do this resume section. When you are done completing this activity, mark this lesson as completed, and meet me in our next lesson, which is Lesson 08 Other Relevant Sections.

WB22

You can go straight to the Functional Resume Master Worksheet and add your 'work history' related details directly to your worksheet. Or, if you prefer, you can complete the Optional Activity below first.

Optional Activity

If you would like, use the space in the three tables below (12.2 to 12.4) to create a master list of all your previous employment and informal work, so you have a record you can refer to in the future. Once you are done, you can then combine the separated out lists into one listing in the Master Worksheet.

Formal Work (Employment (paid work), Self-Employment, Agency work)
12.2

Position Title	Company Name	Started (Month & Year	Finished (Month & Year)

Informal Work (Voluntary Work, Work Experience, Community Participation)

12.3

Position Title	Company Name	Started (Month & Year	Finished (Month & Year)

Personal Situations

12.4

Position Title	Company Name	Started (Month & Year	Finished (Month & Year)

BONUS TUTORIAL

Student Question: – *I am a School Leaver* [or have never worked in a paid role before for some other reason]. *Do I still need to include this section if I have never held a paid position before?*

Team Savvy Answer:

The short answer is yes.

The longer answer is, as I mentioned in the lesson, we want to ensure our resume is as effective as we can possibly make it, and because we have listed relevant skills for the job in our core skills resume section, we next need to anchor those details to a specific place or circumstance where we developed them.

To not include this type of section would become a noticeable curiosity for hiring managers reviewing applications, because half of the information pertaining to the skill is missing – with noticeable curiosities often leading the hiring manager to see the negatives about the application and applicant.

In the business world, you often hear the maxim 'if you don't stand out, you're invisible.' So we have most people and businesses competing to 'be different, so that they become noticed'.

But, the team here at The Savvy Jobseeker Academy and my own self strongly believe that the truer and easier way to stand out and impress is to deliver exactly on the service and delivery expectations of your intended audience or customer, and then fulfil all promises made or inferred.

The process is simple: when you deliver what the customer expects, the customer goes away happy; and when the customer goes away happy, they are willing to tell people about their positive experience, which drives more business to that business and means the business is not invisible, as other customers approach seeking to gain what they expect too and then leave happy, perpetuating an ongoing cycle.

Fail to meet the expectation or deliver on the promises, and the customer goes away unhappy, they are willing to tell people about their negative experience, to protect other people from getting the same unhappy result or wasting their money. Because they haven't stood out for positive reasons, they become just another business in a sea of other businesses, which makes them invisible.

The way for every person and business to successfully stand out was to do what was expected and promised.

So, when it comes to writing our resume, the way to 'be different' just so that you stand out would be to not include this section at all and thus become a noticeable curiosity; and the way to deliver on the expectations then, which is hiring managers will expect to find a 'work history' type section, is to provide the section.

In practicality terms, if you developed your skills as part of an educational course or training (involving theory and testing), then you would anchor those details in your education section listing; otherwise, as discussed in the work history lesson tutorials, the best way to include practical and hands on skill development gained from workplace and workplace-like situations into your resume is to give this section an alternative title.

When the hiring manager sees your different section title, you will cause them to adjust their expectation of what details they will find in the section won't just be your paid work history, but also your non-paid employment based places or situations, such as voluntary work, work experience, community participation or personal pursuits – thus delivering on their expectation that they will find the section, but personalised with a wider background than they had been expecting. All you have done is leverage the section to enhance their continuing to see your suitability and capability.

LESSON 08.

OTHER (POSSIBLY RELEVANT) SECTIONS

Other (Possibly Relevant) SECTIONS

So far in this course we have dealt with each of the essential must-include resume sections (and the optional career objective section). And right now, you could just call creating your resume content quits to go and start building your electronic version if you wanted to, and that would be perfectly okay because all the essential information is covered.

But, for many of you, there could well be a few nice-to-know extras that, if included, may help the hiring manager to further see your suitability for the role even further.

So in this lesson's tutorials, and with the firm reminder that we don't want or need to tell employers everything about ourselves and our abilities, we will now look at some of the most common optional sections jobseekers often include in their resume, to work out whether you might need any of them for your resume.

The Other Possible Relevant Sections we will cover are:

- Referees and References
- Achievements and Awards
- Tools of the Trade
- Computers, Technology & Social Media Savviness
- Hobbies and Personal Interests
- Photos, pictures and other fanciness

TUTORIAL 01. REFEREES AND REFERENCES

As mentioned in previous lessons, employers will never just accept your word about what your employability and suitability is. Interested employers, if considering you for their vacancy, will want and seek out the opinions of independent people and sources to help them fact-check and gain a better (and sometimes more accurate) picture of what you are like as a person and worker before they'll ever take the risk of offering you the job.

And, regardless of whether you agree with employers doing their background checks or not, you can help the employer with their contacting independent people and sources so that the picture they form is consistent with the one you want them to make about you. So this is where a Referees and References section comes into play.

You could provide the details of your referees to them, upfront in your resume; but in modern job-applying practices, it is not compulsory to do this. Actually, it is now often warned against.

The reasons are that there are both pros and cons to including or omitting the Referees and References section.

On the pro side, including details about your referees' means firstly, the reviewing hiring managers can immediately see that you have independent people prepared to vouch for you (which will leave them with a favourable opinion, maybe enough for you to advance to the next stage in their hiring process), and secondly, the employer has all the details on hand for when they are ready to contact your referees (so, again, brownie-points for making life easier for the hiring manager through no delays in needing to obtain these details from you).

On the con side, by the very nature of you applying to a job you are only ever expressing interest in being considered for the role, and generally employers only reach the reference and other fact checking stage after a job interview once they know more about whether they are still interested in you for their role or not.

So including the details of your referees is premature, takes up valuable resume real estate, and, is actually risky. Because there are a lot of legitimate-looking but fake job advertisements on popular job boards, and you need to be very careful about what information you give out – not just to protect yourself, but also the people prepared to vouch for you – to guard against scams and identity theft.

And of course, by not including this section or the specifics, you risk the hiring manager assuming you don't have referees and therefore your likeability factor immediately drops.

But one of the biggest annoyance factors for hiring managers when it comes to resumes is when applicants 'half-provide' information and or resort to the use of trite actions or cliché phrasing to avoid providing particular information upfront.

So, you need to be very clear with your decision to either include or exclude this section, and then follow through on and stick to that decision made.

What I mean here is if you decide to include this section, then you will need to follow through and stick to the rules for including this section; if you decide you won't include this section then you need to follow through on that by leaving out the section and its specifics entirely.

Do not, not, not include the section, but then don't provide the specifics – which an alarming number of jobseekers do, or your application is likely to be rejected.

In other words, don't include a Referees section and then use the words, 'Available upon Request' or other similarly worded phrases.

That is half-providing the details. It's wishy-washy decision making. It's a redundant action, because of course you will provide the details on request, or your application would be terminated immediately.

I don't know who first introduced that wide-spread practice, but it was really poor advice and a really terrible practice that needs to be broken. Because now, it is what people with no referees use as a way of trying to disguise their not having any referees.

Remember, hiring managers know the tricks! So, your decision is straight forward; either include the section or don't include it. It's that simple.

Now, I suggest that if the employer is a government department or well known reputable company, then you will have more reason to provide the details upfront than to not include them; but if the business is smaller and the more it is unknown to you and others, then you should protect your information by not including this section.

But, regardless of whether you include the section in your resume or not, you must have referees and references, and need to be ready to hand the details over when the employer asks for them, during or after the job interview.

And for that reason, we believe you should create a separate document (that is styled exactly the same as your resume) that contains just the details of your referees, so that you can print it out to take with you to the job interview, or have ready and waiting to be forwarded to a potential employer when they request your referee details.

Now, the words Referee and Reference are often used interchangeably, and for the remainder of this tutorial though, I'll just use the word references to make discussing everything easier, but I want to first clarify the difference between them, so you understand what referees and references are.

A referee is a person willing to provide verbal testimonial in support of your inferred promises and stated claims you made about yourself and your capabilities in your application; and references are the testimonials provided in written or verbal form. In other words, a referee is the person, and a reference is what the person supplies – either verbally or in writing.

Written references, sometimes called Letters of Recommendation, should never be included as part of your resume or job application; but they make great items for a Personal Portfolio which you can take with you to a job interview in an attractive display folder for if the employer would like to view your portfolio and or take copies of items of interest.

So this Referees and References section lesson is mainly about providing the details of your Referees.

Now, another thing to take into account is that your references can be either professional or personal in their nature.

When employers ask for references, they generally are asking for professional references because employers view these references as more trustworthy and credible, and therefore more reliable, as a fact-checking source.

Specifically, Professional Referees are the people you know from previous employment and skill development. Potential employers prefer former bosses, managers, supervisors and other leaders or co-workers in positions of authority rather than co-workers working at the same position level as you previously held.

The reason for this is that generally these are the people who understand how business works, are not people in your close-friendship circle (though you may get to know them well during your working or work-like relationship) and have witnessed you within a workplace or workplace-like situation from a business perspective. Therefore, they can provide the firsthand, independent perspective about your skills, attitudes, strengths, capabilities and weaknesses that employers are after. And, ultimately, these are the people who have the most influence towards vouching that you can do the job, do it well, and able to convince the employer that it is okay for them to take the risk in hiring you or not.

And for this reason, for every position you ever hold, try to ensure you get on with your supervisors and leave the job on good terms, because you never know when you will need them to act as a referee for you.

Personal references, on the other hand, are people you know, who you have never worked with (or for), that could be family, friends, acquaintances or community members who are prepared to vouch for you from a personal perspective.

They are usually part of your close-friendship circle and can only provide testimony as to your personality, characteristics, values and ethics because they know you well or for a long time. But, they are in no position to discuss workplace skill levels and capabilities, so they don't have anywhere near the same level of influence as what professional referees do.

Most employers will require the details or 2 or 3 professional referees for adults, and 2 professional referees for school students and school leavers. So, this is another reason why I encouraged you to expand your work history and skill development list to more than just paid positions held. These workplace-like situations are where you can provide some professional referees that you might never have otherwise considered.

It is both common courtesy and best practice to gain permission from each person that you would like to act as a referee for you before providing their contact details so they are not taken by surprise from an unexpected phone call or email, and you know they will be happy to act as referee.

And, you will want to be quite certain that the people you choose actually do hold you in as high regard and will be as supportive about you as you believe they will be.

If you can, then it would be great to have a referee from each companies / workplace-like situations you have listed in your 'work history' type section whatever you called it, for at least the last 5 years worth of positions as a minimum.

Use your best discretion to decide if you wish to include this resume section or not.

So, what if you decide to include this section in your functional resume. What details do you include?

Firstly, entitle the section as either Referees or References – it doesn't matter which one, and then provide the following background details for each of your referees:

- Their name (bolded)
- Position Title
- Company
- Contact phone number or email address (only one contact method is required)

And optionally, especially if the referee may be difficult to get a hold of:

- Best time to contact

And, if the referee has moved on from the role or company:

- Former position title and or company name

Stylistically, depending on how much room you have in your resume to accommodate including this section, you could list the details in any of the following ways:

As a single-line entry.

For example:

- **Joe Bloggs**, Manager, ABC Company Pty Ltd,   0411 119 922
- **Jane Doe**, Managing Director, ZYX Business, 0410 600 900

As a multi-line, dual column entry.

For example:

Joe Blogs	**Jane Doe**
Manager	Managing Director
ABC Company Pty Ltd	ZYX Business
0411 119 922	0410 600 900

As a multiline, single column entry.

For example:

Joe Bloggs
Manager
ABC Company Pty Ltd
0411 119 922

Jane Doe
Managing Director
ZYX Business
0410 600 900

If you will be providing best time to contact information, then the place to add this is after the phone number. If you need to provide a referees former position title or company, then this would be added after the current position title and or company name.

Now, I know I said earlier that it is bad practice to 'half-provide information in a resume. But, there is one, acceptable 'half-providing details' method which employers to see you have referees but which simultaneously allows you to keep the contact specifics secure until you are satisfied that it is safe to provide them that you could use if you wish. That is to list the referees:

- Name,
- Position Title, and
- Company

But leave out only their contact phone number or email address.

If you use this alternative method, then you, too, will need to create a separate document – like those who choose not to include this section; and it would be best to take a print out of the full details with you to the job interview.

Now, reference checks aren't the only checks that hiring managers' carry out to gain an independent perspective about potential candidates. They could also do, as standard hiring practice:

- Criminal history checks
- Qualifications and licensing checks
- Social media and online presence research
- Credit checks (mainly for positions in the accounting and finance industry)

Some employers also require candidates to undergo pre-employment and or regular during employment:

- Drug and alcohol screening
- Physical exams, and or
- Skills and knowledge testing

As a last key point for this lesson, if you decide to include a references section in your resume, then it should be the very last section that you include.

So, for a 1-page resume, it will be the last section towards the bottom of the first page, and for 2-page resumes, it will be the last section on the second page.

The Referees and References section

Keep a record of the people who can or might agree to act as a referee for you

Professional

13.1

Name	
Position Title	
Company	
Phone / Email	

Name	
Position Title	
Company	
Phone / Email	

Name	
Position Title	
Company	
Phone / Email	

Name	
Position Title	
Company	
Phone / Email	

Name	
Position Title	
Company	
Phone / Email	

If you will be including this section in your resume, you can transfer the names of 2 or 3 professional referees into the space provided in the Functional Resume Master Worksheet. (Make sure you have their permission first!)

Personal
13.2

Name	
Position Title	
Company	
Phone / Email	

Name	
Position Title	
Company	
Phone / Email	

BONUS CONTENT

What can referees discuss?

This will depend on the country you live in, but in general, the hiring manager and referee are only permitted to discuss factual details about you.

The factual information they can discuss broadly includes:

- Whether the referee believes you would be suitable to the vacancy
- What you strengths and weaknesses are, and your effectiveness and performance level within the past role was
- How you got along with other people – colleagues, managers and customers
- How you deal with situations like working under pressure, or meeting deadlines
- Your leadership and management abilities
- Your technical ability and skill level, and any areas you need to improve upon
- Your reasons for leaving – as in did you leave of your own accord or were you terminated and why
- Your honesty, integrity and punctuality
- Whether the referee would rehire you

What can't a referee discuss?

Broadly, they cannot discuss anything that could be discriminatory (such as asking what your marital status or sexual preferences might be), or could be slanderous (like, 'they are ugly and mean').

Referees need to be cautious against revealing specific factual details that are not already known to the employer, or could be perceived as their breaching privacy laws through inadvertently disclosing personal information that you have not told them.

TUTORIAL 02. AWARDS & ACHIEVEMENTS

The next optional section that you could include in your functional resume to help convince potential employers of your suitability to the vacancy is a dedicated Awards and Achievements sections.

Now, if you have followed the advice we have given you in this course, then you will have already written quality skill and or personal attribute statements to demonstrate your accomplishment with your skills. So I'll say upfront: you may not need to create an additional section to demonstrate your higher performance and accomplishments.

But, if you have awards or special achievements relating to the type of work you seek to gain, which you haven't been able to get into your resume already (because you don't want to destroy the effectiveness of your resume by repeating the same information), then creating this section is the ideal way for you able to get this additional information in.

The types of awards and special achievements that you could include need to still be relevant to the type of work you are seeking to gain, so things like having been named employee or salesperson of the month, having received bonus pay or gift cards in recognition of higher performance, or even just praise or feedback received from managers as a result of you doing a particular duty or task better than everyone else that had them raving about you is potential fodder for this section.

But, where possible, try to make the specifics that you include show a picture of on-going achievement too. What I mean here, is you need to avoid creating a picture that shows you had past success but those glory-moments stopped a few years ago.

Another thing to be careful of here is that unless you are creating a resume for educational reasons such as to gain a scholarship, you don't want to include too many educational-based achievements. It is important to remember that the reason you are creating a resume is because you are applying for a job, so as much as possible you want the achievements you showcase to be workplace gained or related, such as achievement from your performance in carrying out tasks or the practical use of your skills, rather than for passing tests or completed assignments.

Finally, like you do for other sections list the specifics in bullet form and give your section a relevant title. This section is a good replacement for the Referees & References section. Ending your resume on such a positive note could help to leave a strong positive impression in the hiring manager about you and your application; otherwise, you could position the section in the PRRE to help kick off forming a good impression.

Awards & Achievements

Keep a record of the relevant awards and achievements you have that are relevant to the type of work you seek to gain

Awards

13.4

Award Name	
Issued by	
Significance	

Award Name	
Issued by	
Significance	

Award Name	
Issued by	
Significance	

Award Name	
Issued by	
Significance	

You can now add these details to the Functional Resume Master Worksheet.

Achievements

13.5

Achievement	

Achievement	

Achievement	

Achievement	

If you have other relevant sections that you would like to include (e.g. Tools of the Trade), please add them directly into the Functional Resume Master Worksheet. Remember to give the section a suitably section title.

TUTORIAL 03. TOOLS OF THE TRADE

In some job roles, you may need to use specialised tools or machinery, and when you are already proficient in using that equipment, it can be beneficial to let potential employers know this.

Now, the Tools of the Trade section started out as a section for those seeking work in the building and construction industry, where there are often similar job titles that have position holders completing different types of tasks (e.g. 'labourer' roles). But this section can be useful for school leavers, career changers and parents returning to the paid workforce too, because it enables them to demonstrate their non-workplace acquired tools and equipment proficiency.

Again, you need to decide on the appropriateness to include such a section in your resume; and consider the needs of the job role to ensure the details are relevant to what you are seeking to gain. For example, there is no value to be gained by listing, say, the various kitchen tools you are proficient with if you are applying for a forklift driving role; but listing the kitchen equipment would have added value if you were applying for a cook or other kitchen assistant position.

If you decide that including a Tools of the Trade type section would be beneficial, then you just need to create a simple bullet listing. For example, and office worker might list:

- Comb binder
- Laminator
- Fax machine
- Office guillotine
- Cash register

Depending on how many entries you have in your list, you could style your bullet list into single or multiple columns, and you can call the section whatever you like, such as Tools & Equipment, or Office Equipment, Equipment Snapshot.

If you include this section, then the best place to position the section is after your core skills section but before your work history type section – to keep the summary of skills and abilities appearing on the page before readers are anchored to where they were gained. That is, our claims and promises come before our factual background.

TUTORIAL 04. COMPUTERS, TECHNOLOGY & SOCIAL MEDIA SAVVINESS

Computers & Technology

Technology is prevalent within our modern society; so there is an employer expectation that workers can operate computers and gadgetry on at least a basic level (such as knowing how to turn the computer or device on). But, if you need to bring attention to specific computer programs you are proficient in or that you possess particular advanced level skills with, then this would be the section to create so you can highlight those details.

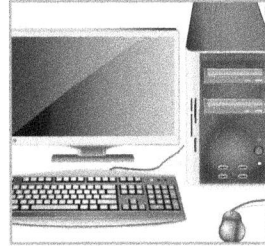

Now, although computers and gadgetry could indeed be considered Tools of the Trade, we gave this resume section a tutorial of its own because while the Tools of the Trade is ideal for those attempting to gain a particular role for the first time to highlight how they can already use the tools and equipment needed in the role to help you to gain entry to the type of work that uses that equipment, the computers and technology section is more about showcasing your area of expertise to give you a competitive edge against those who don't have these higher skill levels.

For example, a beginner typist might be able to type at the basic rate of 35 wpm, and an experience typist might have built her speed through experience up to 70 or 100 wpm. The advantage of highlighting this higher skill level is the experienced typist can type double or triple the workload volume compared to the beginner typist. In some positions that will matter, in others it won't.

The same sort of advantage exists for those who are proficient in the use of one computer program over another.

Therefore, the decision to include a computer and technology section fully depends on whether the job you seek to gain involves using computers and technology or not, and whether highlighting your computer prowess will also show your increased value.

If you decide that including a computers and technology section would be beneficial, then you just need to create a simple bullet listing also, and give the section an appropriate title.

There are a number of different styling options including providing a plain listing to keep the section consistent in style to the other resume sections, or graphically indicating your ability level either through use of the words 'intermediate' or 'advanced', or through subtle graphical representation, like a visual star rating or graph.

You will need to decide whereabouts on your resume will be the best place to position your section. The more important the specifics are for the type of job you seek to gain, then the higher up the resume your section needs to be positioned. For example, if your computer and technology details are the most important factor, say, like a Graphic Designer needing to list which computer programs they are proficient with, then you might position your section before your core skills section. But, if your computer and technology details are just supportive of your core skills then you would position them after your core skills section but before your work history type section like you do for the Tools of the Trade section.

Again, you will need to choose an appropriate title, like Computers & Technology, or Programs, depending on the details including in the listing.

Social Media Savviness

The other thing to consider is your social media savviness. These days, large portions of the population have personal social media accounts and therefore have developed some useful social media skills, which many businesses are looking for.

If you just use Facebook or Twitter to just talk to family and friends, and perhaps sharing the latest meme's and viral posts doing the rounds, then your social media savviness is unlikely to be necessary for highlighting in your resume.

But, if you have a side-line business, or hobby blog etc, then you may well want to get this into your resume if it will give you an advantage for the type of work you seek to gain.

Some aspects relating to social media savviness that you could include are:

- Number of site visits (to your blog or website)
- Number of followers or subscribers (to your profiles, pages, accounts and posts)
- The frequency with which you post
- The range of products you've sold online, and frequency of sales (e.g. running an Ebay, Etsy or similar store)
- The type of content you create (e.g. blog posts, podcasts, videos, screencasts, eBooks, infographics, sales landing pages, courses etc.)
- The platforms you use
- The budget levels you work to
- The promotions and campaigns you have initiated / managed to completion
- The tools and programs you use to track and monitor your resumes (e.g. analytics, keyword research, spreadsheets, databases etc)

As with the computers and technology section, where you position the section will depend on how important the information is for the role being sought, and you could personalise the section in the variety of ways already discussed earlier.

TUTORIAL 05. HOBBIES & PERSONAL INTERESTS

We discuss this additional resume section only because we want to save students from emailing us to ask about it thinking we have missed an important section accidentally.

We don't use a Hobbies & Personal Interest type section for any of our clients as we prefer to draw out and highlight the key employability skills our clients have rather than their hobbies, interests and personal past times which are more often than not irrelevant to the job, and therefore unnecessary.

We think you should probe your employability skills more deeply too, and leave this section as an absolute last resort only for if you are low on direct skills and experiences for the type of job you seek to gain and other details to include in your resume – and even then, only include the section and provide details that will give your application a little boost towards helping the hiring manager to see your suitability. But, that doesn't happen very often.

The reason I am blatantly discouraging the use of this section is because, and I've discussed this before in this course, of the need to not make our resumes too much about who we are or how we live our personal lives to instead make it more employment focused. And, because every hobby or personal interest has both a positive and negative side to it, making the details dangerously 'double-edged'.

Take for example reading. Seems harmless enough, doesn't it.

But, let's examine that personal activity closer.

Unless you are reading aloud to someone else, like a child, reading is usually a solo-pursuit. A quiet, relaxing personal past time.

Most hiring managers are looking for how well the person will fit in with their business and how well they will get along with their existing workers; so they will be more in the mind frame of looking for examples of team work and collaborating.

Telling employers that reading is one of your hobbies or personal interests then outrightly conflicts with what the employer is after. Sure, it can imply that you have good written communication skills – because people who love reading usually have a good command of the English language, but if the employer isn't thinking about your needing good written communication skills – and frankly they are on open display already – what you are left with is a conflict that lowers the effectiveness of your application. Because, instead of seeing you as someone who values team work, the message you've inadvertently sent is that you like to get away from others and do things on your own.

So, when might reading match the needs of the job role and hiring manager expectation? Yes, that's right, if the person is applying for a position in a library, where their love of books and or reading aloud would be useful in the workplace – because they would be able to talk to library patrons about different books they've read, or might enjoy hosting children's story time.

Unfortunately, most jobseekers don't think deeply enough about the specifics they include or consider the impact the details have upon how the hiring manager ultimately views them. Every single word that goes in your resume has to be there for a reason; and its presence is then open to interpretation and judgement. So if you are going to include a hobbies and personal interests section in your resume, you need to pay careful attention to each and every specific, and consider not just the positive aspects but also what negatives the hiring manager can derive from it.

I suggest that if you do include a hobbies and personal interest section in your resume, that you position it after your core skills section but before your work history type section. I don't recommend leaving it as the last resume section, to prevent the hiring manager ending on a possible negative value judgement.

TUTORIAL 06. PHOTOS, PICTURES & OTHER FANCINESS

In this tutorial I'm going to cover the use of photos, pictures and other fancy elements. I'll start with a commonly asked question of 'Is it okay to include a photo in your resume?'

The answer to that is no.

A resume is a document that outlines your skills and experiences. It is not a Personal dossier.

When you apply to a job, you want the hiring manager to consider you based solely on your ability to do the job and do it well, nothing else. With the exception of some lines of work, like acting, you don't want their decision to be based on how you look, or how old you are.

Photographs reveal both.

During the application stage, employers just want to receive a bunch of anonymous applications, as in, they are just names on paper, so they can sift through reviewing those applications to find the best candidates.

Receiving resumes with a photograph is jarring because the photograph takes away that anonymity aspect. Always remember there is a time and place for everything – a logical sequence of progression. When employers are ready to put a face to the name they are interested in, they call them in and invite them in to a job interview.

Designer Resumes

The next fanciful element I want to discuss is Designer Resumes, which seem to be all the rage with jobseekers right now.

I've noticed that a number of Graphic Designers offer resume services to jobseekers, and they tell jobseekers that the 'trick' to getting your resume read is to create 'designer', 'creative' or otherwise visually eye-catching resumes, as the only way for jobseekers to stand out.

I agree, those resumes do stand out. But, not necessarily in a positive way or the way you want.

As I've mentioned before, the only real way to impress the hiring manager is to address what is wanted, needed and expected in the job role, and presentation trickery isn't the way to achieve that.

Those Graphic Designers sales pitches are just that: sales pitches to drum up sales that keep them in business.

Do they have hiring experience? Most don't. Actually, some of the graphic designers I saw advertising were fresh out of design school and looking for employment themselves, and were offering their resume services as a side-hustle.

I understand why their sales pitches work though; having a beautiful document is way more enticing to look at than an ugly-looking document but let me tell you a little personal story.

A number of years ago, when I was first learning about resume writing, I came across those sorts of graphic designer sales pitches and because I had the word processing skills and didn't have any hiring experience at that point, rather than engage in their services, I decided to create a 'designer' looking resume for my own self to use because I wanted to obtain a part time job.

Now, I have to admit, I completely surprised myself with how beautiful my resume turned out – I used a beautiful purple onscreen that when I printed the document out, appeared as a different but delightfully eye-catching 'silvery' beige instead. I used a beautiful script font for my name and the section titles, and a light complementing sans serif font for the rest of the text that gave the resume an elegant but feminine look. I used fanciful bullet points and inserted rectangles into the header and footer shape-filled with the same purple to bring cohesiveness to my design.

My only trouble was, although I had plenty of relevant skills to do the job type I was applying to, I was lacking one key skill that employers valued, so I knew I was going to have a hard time getting beyond that barrier to gain a job offer. I naively thought my designer resume might do the trick.

I applied to about 25 jobs with that resume; and I received a phone call from every single one, inviting me in for an interview. That sounds like a good thing, right? Wrong.

Instead, I learned a valuable lesson.

The very first thing those employers told me was they weren't going to consider me for the role (thus leaving me to wonder, *'well, why did you get me to come in then?'* I soon gained the answer to that wonderment too when they told me they had just got me to come in so that they could meet the person who had sent them such a beautiful resume.

Did you create it yourself, how long did it take you? they asked. You have really good skills; I love that 'silvery-beige colour!' they complimented. And, probably because it was a job in the employment services industry, each hiring manager told me I should explore a career in graphic design or desktop publishing!

But, despite my obviously have some fantastic relevant skills that would help in that type of job and my obvious want to gain this particular type of work to be worthy of consideration, instead I got, we won't hire you until you have the case management skill you are missing, so, please, thank you for coming in and don't hesitate to contact us again in the future when you do have case management experience, but please, you really should think about getting into desktop publishing.

It was so damn annoying!

I was applying to part time jobs because I wanted steady income while I still worked for myself as a typist / document creator because self employment income could be quite sporadic, but, attending job interviews where they were never going to offer me the job, or even consider it was unnecessarily costing me money and time.

To be honest, I would have rather have received a rejection letter!

Did those hiring managers mean to waste my time and money only to tell me I'm not what they are looking for yet? Not intentionally, no. They believed they were doing me a favour. Were they paying attention to any of the fully relevant skills and experiences I did have for that type of job? No, they were too focused on how I had presented my resume content.

So, the reason I've shared that story with you is because I later went on to gain a role where I was the hiring manager, and, I had a few designer resumes land in my fax machine too, that I cooed and cahhed over. But like I was, most of you are applying to non-creative roles; and what the hiring manager actually values is the person's skills, experiences and capabilities for the job role.

It is what those hiring managers that interviewed me wanted and expected; it's what I wanted and expected when I reviewed applications. And, I personally never had a jobseeker who had submitted a designer resume to our agency progress to their being the applicant suitable for the job – it was as though they had gone all fancy in their design to make up for their having poor content or a lack of experience, which when you think about it is the mistake I had made. I stood out for the wrong reasons, and hiring managers failed to see my other relevant skills and experiences because of that, which stopped when I went back to a plain, professional resume.

So let me be clear: plain, professional resumes with a focus on the content and how it demonstrates your suitability to the role works best for non-creative roles. There are plenty of hiring managers online that say this.

And, for those of you who are attempting to gain a creative-natured role, then it is your design skills and abilities which need to be demonstrated in your applications, not those that belong to someone else.

Another reason why I don't encourage Designer Resumes is because often they are created using Adobe InDesign or Photoshop and issued as a PDF document, to prevent the design from being copied.

Not all hiring managers want, or their systems won't allow them, to receive PDF documents. Think about it, you spend a fortune to get a designer resume, and it later needs changes made and it will cost you to get it updated. And what do these jobseekers do when the job advertisement specifies that applicants should forward their resume in Microsoft Word or Rich Text Format? Which are the 2 most commonly requested formats because they are the most compatible for recruiters Applicant Tracking Software.

Finalise with
FINESSE
MODULE

Post-Lesson
Basics

01.

BONUS: FUNCTIONAL FORMAT RESUME TEMPLATE

01. BONUS: Functional Format Resume TEMPLATE

Just because you have purchased the print version doesn't mean you should miss out getting the Microsoft Word Template that we have provided to our online students.

So, to receive your copy of the already formatted Resume Template that matches up to the Functional Resume Master Worksheet found at the rear of this book, please visit the print book blog at:

http://createafunctionalresume.blogspot.com.au/p/cfr.html

Both 1-page and 2-page templates are available.

We remind you, though, that only people who have purchased this print publication have permission to use the template for their own personal use, and the template is not for sharing or distribution.

TUTORIAL 01. THE BONUS WORD TEMPLATE

We understand that not everyone who takes this course has the higher computer skills needed to create their electronic document, especially when it comes to much of the formatting. So, to make things easier for you, we have created a Microsoft Word template, which you can use as the basis to creating your electronic file, if you'd like.

We decided to provide you with a Microsoft Word template, rather than a document, so that there is less chance of those with lower word-processing skills messing up the existing formatting, and so that you can create your electronic document in the quickest time possible.

But there are a couple of points to mention about this bonus resource:

Firstly, as I said, Team Savvy has provided you with a Microsoft Word template. That means that when you double click on the file icon after downloading it to your computer, your computer will open a document based on the template. Any changes to the text that you make are made to the document you've created, not the template. Once you've made changes, you will need to save the document with an appropriate file name – for advice on this, please watch the Tutorial 03 of this lesson below this one.

It is important that you do not Right Click on the icon and then choose Open; otherwise you will be altering the template itself. We suggest you leave the template as is, so that you can re-use it later if necessary. And we remind you that this resource permits you to use it for your sole personal use only, and that it is unlawful for you to share it or any of the other resources from this course with other people or distribute it by any means.

So let's assume that you've downloaded the template, double-clicked on the icon and now have the document waiting for you.

The first thing we recommend is that you save the document as the very first thing you do, so that it has an appropriate file name. From this point forward, if you don't finish creating your resume in this updating it sitting, you would simply come back to this Word document file (which is now your 'Base Resume') instead of the resume template we provided (which is now your 'Electronic Master Resource').

Now, with the files part sorted, all you need to do next is start methodically working your way from top to bottom of the document in conjunction with the Functional Resume Master Worksheet at the back of your Student Workbook that you have filled out; each time highlighting only the portion of the sample text provided in the template that you wish to change and replace it with your own, before rinsing and repeating the process.

For example, in the Personal Details section, where the text states 'Name Surname' you would highlight just the words 'Name Surname' and then overwrite the text with your particular first name and surname. Once successfully completed, you would then move on to the next line of text which says Email and overwrite the placeholder text with the email address you will be using throughout your jobsearch.

The next thing I want to discuss is we have labelled the different resume sections for you. You'll notice that we have entitled those sections the same as we did in the Functional Resume Master Worksheet. And, we remind you that you can change these Section Headlines to something more appropriate or better suited to your personal preferences too.

Finally, you will need to be really careful not to mess up the formatting as you work. We encourage you to use the same character formatting that we have used. That is, if we have used all capital letters (known as All Caps), then you should replace the text using all capitals. If we have used all lowercase letters, then you replace the text using all lowercase. And, when we've used Sentence case, which means it has a combination of Capitalised letters and lower case, then you need to follow the proper rules of Grammar to capitalise words, in particular nouns, where appropriate.

TUTORIAL 02. PERSONALISING YOUR RESUME DOCUMENT

If you do not like the font typeface and size etc, then you are free to personalise the formatting to something you like better. However, it is important to ensure that you keep elements consistent.

What I mean is, if you say decided to change the Core Skills Section Headline to the font Garamond at size 13 point, then you would need to change each of the other Section Headlines to the same character formatting. You could use the Format Painter tool to do this quickly, or go through each Section Heading and change to your preferences manually.

Please keep in mind that the main purpose in creating your resume is not to get fancy but to convert the hiring manager from skim-reading to actual reading. The more embellishments and stylising you do to your Base Resume, the more you risk causing the Hiring Manager to notice you for the wrong, negative reasons.

TUTORIAL 03. FILE NAME

Once you have created a document from the electronic master template we have provided to you, you will need to save the document with an appropriate file name so that you can find it again in the future, and so that hiring managers can find it on their computers too.

For this reason, please do not save your resume with the file name resume.doc. That might end up as the only document with that file name on your computer, but you would be surprised by how many employers receive with that file name.

When I worked as a Marketer for one employment service agency, I went out on the field and found employers needing staff and then came back to the office and broadcast the vacancy and the requirements to the case managers in 4 local branches, who would each review their caseload of jobseeking client and then email me back the resumes of those that matched the requirements, that is the person had the skills and were job ready. And you would be surprised by how many resumes sent through had the filename resume. doc.

I immediately had to waste my time renaming the files to the particular jobseekers name, just so that I could store the resume in a folder on my laptop hard drive and could later just search that folder to quickly and easily open or forward the correct one.

So please make sure you save your resume with a filename that will be meaningful to the employer or other recipient. That is, save your document with your name. For example, Char Mesan.doc or even Char Mesan Resume.doc.

I personally don't bother including the word resume in the file name, because I like to date my resumes with the month we are in, which has a positive effect of showing the hiring managers who receive it that the resume is current. For example, Char Mesan_ September2015.doc. I don't want to the file name to become too long, which is why I don't bother with the word resume.

Now, if you will be applying to multiple types of job roles to maximise your changes of gaining a job more quickly, which is a perfectly reasonable and acceptable jobsearch practice, you will need to create a base resume for each type of job role though. And of course, by having multiple resumes on your computer or storage device, it can become easy to accidently sent off the wrong one.

The way to make it easier for you to send the right resume is to add the job type into the file name. For example

> Char Mesan_Jobsearch Trainer_September2015 or Char Mesan_
> Proofreader_September2015.

Finally, I recommend that you have a dedicated folder on your computer hard drive or storage device where you keep copies of your resume, cover letters and other application and electronic keepsakes. You never know when you might need to relook at what you previously sent. Actually, a good jobsearch practice is to review the application your submitted if you are invited to an interview to reacquaint yourself with exactly what you said within that application!

02.

REVISE AND POLISH **TO CAPTIVATE**

TUTORIAL 01. CHECK FOR COMPLETENESS

Now that you have written the content for your resume and created the electronic version, I want you to look over your resume and try to see things from a Hiring Managers perspective. Knowing what you do about the job role you will be applying to, is your information complete?

That is, do you need to add, delete or alter anything to your resume?

If you do, then please use your best judgement and make your tweaks.

If you don't need to add, delete or alter what you've got, excellent!

TUTORIAL 02. CONSISTENCY

Sometimes when we are creating our electronic file, things don't always go as smoothly as they should, especially when we are overwriting text.

Before you consider your resume done for now, please check your formatting to make sure that all elements have been applied consistently.

That is, check your headings: do each of the headings use the same font, font size, font colour (auto black) and have the same emphasis and or text affects applied to it? And same again with the body text. Is any part not the way it should be?

Well, if there are any inconsistencies, please make sure you fix them up and save the changes.

If everything is as it is meant to be, fantastic! Well done, you.

TUTORIAL 03. SPELL & GRAMMAR CHECK

The last thing you need to do is check that your spelling, punctuation and grammar is correct, especially if this is not your forte. You've worked so hard to ensure your resume will be the most effective it could possibly be so you don't want a trivial thing like typos and silly spelling mistakes to stick out like an eyesore – because that's what happens when people notice a mistake. It looks out of place, and we know it is wrong – and you don't want to irk the hiring manager unnecessarily.

So, head straight over to the Review tab in Microsoft Word – or wherever Spell Check is located for you if you are using a different wordprocessing program like Google Docs or Open Office – and run spell check. It won't catch words that are spelled correctly but wrongly used, but it will help you catch the most obvious spelling, punctuation and grammar errors.

Then, when you are finished, save your document and then print it out. This is a trick that professional editors and proofreaders use to catch errors, because the human reads a document different when viewing on paper compared to onscreen, so it helps us to catch errors we wouldn't have otherwise have noticed.

And, for good measure to make sure your resume is as error free as it can possibly be, please have at least one other person – preferably someone with strong written communication and or proofreading skills – to look over your resume too.

If any mistakes are detected, please make sure you change your template base resume, so that you don't have to keep remembering to change them in a document.

03.

TWEAKING YOUR RESUME LENGTH

TUTORIAL 01. RESUME FORMATTING PRO-TECHNIQUES

Two Useful Tools

Functional Resumes work best when they are either exactly 1-page or exactly 2-page in length. So on the one hand, you want to get all of your custom-written, fully tailored, unique content into your document, but on the other hand, because of this exactness issue, the chances are high (and likely) that you could end up with a document falling somewhere between not quite enough, a single line more than one page, all the way up to having almost 2 pages.

So this lesson is all about using formatting 'tweaks' and pro-techniques to help you reach getting a precise 1 or 2 page document.

Now, you will need to pay around with some of the text and formatting to make things work the way you want, and even more so, you will need to use your discretion as the best way to proceed when you have multiple options that you could try. But at its most basic, the way to make your resume precisely 1 or 2 pages is through either:

1. Adding sections and or section specifics,
2. Removing sections and or section specifics, or
3. Altering the existing appearance of your sections and specifics by adjusting the text, paragraph and or page formatting of your electronic document.

It's not quite as overwhelming as it all sounds.

You'll need to work out whether adding or removing sections is the best way to proceed, but the rest of this lesson's tutorials are about showing you the various common options to achieve point 3 – adjusting the formatting of your text for when that is the best way to proceed.

So let's begin, shall we.

My 2 Most Used Formatting Tools

I'm going to start by telling you about 2 Microsoft Word tools that I use when I create resumes – which I just can't work without. Not just because these tools are personal favourites, but because they are the most useful – and helpful – for a range of uses, too!

The 2 tools are the:

- Format Painter tool, and the
- Pilcrow (Paragraph Marker)

The Format Painter

Microsoft Word opens with default settings for every aspect of creating an electronic document that you could imagine. And formatting is just changing those default settings for the document you are working on – unless you are creating a template, which is when you are setting the defaults for all documents based off that template in the future.

Now, the format painter tool, which is one of many wordprocessing tools Microsoft Word has to offer, is a tool that was designed to help you maintain consistency in your formatting, and to increase your speed and efficiency in performing wordprocessing tasks.

The format painter tool can be found on the Home tab, under the Clipboard ribbon tool grouping. It has an angled paint brush and the words Format Painter as its icon, and feature activator.

The format painter tool is sort of like copy and paste in how it works. Except, instead of copying the text and that text being held in the clipboard so that it can be pasted elsewhere in the same document or in another file on your computer, with the format painter you are only copying the formatting that has been applied to that copied portion of text.

The formatting information is stored in your computer memory while the tool is activated until you 'paint' a different portion of text that you choose to have the same formatting applied to it – which I call the recipient text – with your mouse clicking.

This tool is useful because it saves you time from having to highlight the recipient text to manually when the text has multiple formatting changes applied to it, as the tool then applies every one of those formatting changes made from the copied text formatting to the recipient text.

For example, if you have a section title that you have changed to appear as bold, Size 14, All Caps and centre-aligned (which is multiple formatting changes), and you have another section title that you want to give the exact same formatting too, rather than having to bold the text, change the font size and change to all capital letters, and then centre align it – which is 4 separate formatting processes – instead you could just highlight the correctly formatted section title text, use your mouse to click on the format painter, and then while the tool is activated, highlight the recipient section title. When you release the mouse button, the recipient text automatically changes to the new formatting, thus saving you a little bit of time compared to doing it manually.

But the real bonus time saver is when you have multiple section titles you need to format.

When you single-click on the format painter tool, once you have completed the action to apply the formatting changes, you are done. Task over. But, if you double-click the format painter tool, it keeps the format painting tool actively engaged once you are finished painting a portion of text, so you can go on to reformat other portions text.

Once you are done reformatting text using the Format Painter, you will need to turn the format painting tool off again (or deactivate it) by either clicking on the format painter tool icon again, or, I often do it by formatting another piece of text that I don't want reformatted and then immediately clicking on the Undo button (or else using the Undo keyboard shortcut, which is Control + Z, which is what I more often tend to use).

The Pilcrow

The next useful wordprocessing tool that makes my document creating easy is the Pilcrow.

The Pilcrow, otherwise called the Paragraph Marker in Microsoft Word, is another fantastic tool that I use all the time. I sometimes jokingly call this tool the frustration-resolver!

It is often the secret to my success compared to other users, because when you turn it on, it shows you hidden formatting symbols relating to keystrokes made and or formatting that have been applied. And from that, you can see what is happening behind the scenes to start to identify what is going wrong or possibly causing the problem being experienced.

At first, those symbols might not mean much to you, but once you get familiar with this tool and what the symbols mean, it is really helpful in helping you to resolve problems you are having when you, say, are trying to do one thing but the program keeps doing something else. In almost every occurrence, the cause behind the conflict is because of hidden formatting.

The Pilcrow can be found on the Home tab, in the Paragraph grouping on the ribbon. The icon sort of looks like a backward letter 'P', except with 2 downstrokes instead of one, and instead of a hollow circle, the pilcrow's round part is filled. It is a tiny button that a lot of computers don't even know exists, let alone what it does and how it could help them resolve the issue they're having!

To activate this tool, is simple: you just need to click on the icon once. And to deactivate, you just need to click on the button again, to toggle it off.

The basics of the paragraph markings are:

- The Pilcrow symbol when this tool is activated shows each occurrence of when the Enter key has been used.
- The dots or airborne full stops between each word typed show when the space bar has been use, but when it is a circle instead of a dot, it shows that hard space

has been used instead of normal spacing. (You use a hard space to keep text together, like numbers in a phone number, from being split and the parts falling onto different lines).

- And arrow pointing to the right shows that the tab key has been used to indent,
- When the tool is turned on, you can see where section breaks have been applied
- And, you can see the difference between manually created breaks have been entered compared to text, paragraph or page formatting [show difference between extra Enter versus Space Before or After]

There are other symbols for when the text is in a table, and if you want to learn more about how this tool can help you, then you could start by heading to the Microsoft Word Help file to read up about this feature, and or play around by toggling the feature on and off to work out what it does and doesn't reveal when it is activated, or even head over to a search engine to find articles later, as it is out   of the scope of this course to go into this feature any deeper.

Next time you are having problems getting your document to do what you want it to do, remember to use this tool!

So, thank you for watching. I'll see you in the next tutorial.

TUTORIAL 02. RESUME FORMATTING PRO-TECHNIQUES

Text Hierarchy and Page Formatting

Welcome back. In the first tutorial for resume formatting pro-techniques, I discussed the 3 ways you have to be able to force your resume to become exactly 1 or 2 pages, and then I introduced you to the 2 Microsoft Word tools that I use constantly when creating documents using this program.

In this second tutorial, I'll briefly discuss another useful tool that you could use if you wanted to – though I personally don't use it that often for resumes. And, then we'll move on to the default settings that we just need to check and or make changes to once to get them to how we want them to be.

So let's get into it, shall we.

Styles / Text Hierarchy

Although I rarely use the Styles feature when creating resumes, this wordprocessing tool exists and is infrequently used by some jobseekers, because the feature is mainly used for longer documents, and desktop publishing. I'm mentioning it though because not only is there nothing wrong with your using the Styles feature, if you would like to use it, but also because if you activate the Pilcrow, you'll see that we have created a Style and entitled it as Heading 3, and we have applied that style to each of the Section titles.

So, the Styles feature operates on the concept that documents and text have a textual hierarchy. That is, some text is more important, or carries more weight, than other pieces of text.

You could apply hierarchy to your text, and then change the look and feel without needing to use the format painter tool or go through and make the changes manually, because when you change that hierarchy's Style or formatting, it will apply to every piece of text that you've assigned to that particular hierarchy level. So, it is a super time saver tool when working with publications and longer documents.

Now, when you open a document and start typing, unless you tell the computer otherwise, you are typing the text and simultaneously applying 'normal text' hierarchy and formatting style to it. But, you could change the hierarchy, for say a Section title to 'Heading' style, and that will change the formatting to that particular heading style and leave all other text alone.

The trouble is, there aren't very many pre-set Styles in Microsoft Word and most users don't know how to create their own, so that small range of preset designs have become overused.

So, if you are going to use Styles, then you would be better off creating your own unique Style than use one of the presets. Just be aware, that setting up Styles can take a while; and if you don't know what you are doing, the Styles menu can end up becoming a bit of a mess.

It is out of the scope of this course and tutorial to teach you how to create your own Styles, but, you will find the Styles feature on the Home tab in the Styles grouping on the ribbon.

Also, you could also just assign hierarchy to your text through either applying a style name (or hierarchy) to your text, or you can go to the References tab, and choose the 'Add text' button under the Table of Contents grouping in the ribbon.

But like I said, being that we are only working with a one or two page document, we don't really need to go to the added effort of applying styles to our formatting – unless you think you might want to just change the look of your resume from time to time, with a simple theme change.

Okay, now let's chat about what default settings we will just be checking but probably won't need to change.

What we won't be adjusting

As I mentioned earlier, the wordprocessing program that you use will come with default settings for every aspect you can think of. And not everything will need to be changed; some default settings will already be exactly how you need them to be.

The 3 things we will check but may not need to change are:

- Paper size
- Page orientation, and
- Language / Dictionary setting

Paper Size and Orientation

My Word documents automatically default to an A4 Page Size using the Portrait orientation, and the Times New Roman font set at Size 12 point every time I open a new document, because I changed the default template, so I don't need to make any adjustments to these settings each time.

But, there are a couple of variants depending on your country of origin.

For example, if you are from the U.S., then your standard paper size for printing, I believe is US Letter, which although is close in size and look to A4 which Australia uses as its standard paper, they are in fact different paper sizes.

So, as best practice, check that the program you are using is correctly defaulting to the paper size for what your country uses, and that the page orientation is set to portrait, unless your country's standard business correspondence uses a Landscape orientation.

To check this in Microsoft Word, go to the Page Layout tab and then separately check the settings under both the Orientation and Size buttons in the tools ribbon. As far as I am aware, all English speaking countries use Portrait orientation for resumes and cover letters, so you will need to change the page orientation to portrait mode if it defaults to landscape mode.

Language

The other thing you will need to check, especially if you are not from the U.S. is that the default language is set to the country you reside in, because English (United States) is often the default language assigned during installation and users from other countries generally end up having to change their language, currency and metric defaults, but for Americans, these defaults are already correctly set.

We aren't too worried about the currency or metrics, here, but because each country has different spellings of words and grammar and punctuation rules – the most notable difference being that Americas spell certain words using the letter 'z' whereas Australian English uses the letter, 's' like the U.K – and we don't want our own selves or hiring managers to mistakenly think we have spelled words correctly when we haven't, and nor do we want our correctly spelled words erroneously being marked by the program as incorrectly spelt simply because the program we are using engages the wrong default dictionary, you should check the defaults are set correctly, especially if it is a public computer that you are using.

To check that you are using the correct default dictionary for your country, you can see what language (and dictionary) the program is set to by viewing this on the bottom taskbar of Microsoft Word.

If you need to make changes to this setting, you can either click on the words to activate a hidden menu, or you can go the Review tab and then under the Proofing tools, click on Set Language.

Okay, with those basics now out of the way, in the next tutorial we will start learning how to make specific formatting adjustments for our resume. So, thank you for watching and I'll see you in the next tutorial.

TUTORIAL 03. PAGE, PARAGRAPH AND TEXT FORMATTING

Welcome back.

In this lesson, we will now start looking at possible ways we can adjust the formatting of our document to stylise and get the end product we are after.

Note: Because we have provided you with a Microsoft Word document template, we will treat that as being the default setting – but this could be different from blank documents you create using that same computer.

So, the Microsoft Word features or formatting options we will look at are:

Page formatting

- Margins
- Columns
- Breaks

Paragraph formatting

- Line Spacing
- Space Before & Space After
- Tabs & Indents

Text formatting

- Font
- Font Size

The first thing I want to discuss is that you can format a document anywhere during the creation process. That is before, during and after opening a document.

Microsoft pre-formatted the blank template which we use to create blank documents so that it was ready for instant typing. But, most users don't want to keep to that formatting, so they are free to just start typing (or importing text) and leave the formatting until the end, or, like most users, to stop and carry out some formatting as and when it arises.

Secondly, formatting falls into one of 3 key areas: text, paragraph and page.

When we apply effects to text, like bolding, underlining or changing the font colour, we are adjusting the formatting on a Text (or Character) Formatting level.

But, when we adjust the columns, breaks, line spacing etc, we are formatting our documents on a Paragraph level.

On its own, each of the different formatting could be what you need to use in order to adjust your resume. Oftentimes you may need to use a combination for adjustments.

I'll start with the Page formatting, move on to the paragraph formatting and then finish off this tutorial with the text formatting options.

Margins

Standard business documents use 2.54 cm (or 1 inch) margins top, bottom and sides.

Now, I encouraged you to write skill statements for some of your section bullet points, so if you end up with text falling onto a second page by only a line or two, then you may be able to get back a 1 page spread by widening the line length, which is achieved by reducing the margins.

Some combinations you could try include:

- Change the bottom margin only to 1.91 cm or 1.27 cm (¾ or ½ inch), leaving the top and side margins as is,
- Change all margins to 1.91 com (¾ inch), or
- Change the sides and bottom margin to 1.91 or 1.27 cam (¾ or ½ inch), leaving only the top margin as is

I don't recommend ever adjusting the top margin to 1.27 (or ½ inch), because it then makes your information too high up on the page, and that looks out of place.

I recommend that you only use the standard 0.63 cm (or ¼ inch) adjustment increments and never go any smaller than 1.27 cm.

Always keep the left and right margins exactly the same as each other; but, the top and bottom margins are allowed to differ from each other. As a general rule, the bottom margin can be smaller than the top, but not the other way around.

We want our adjustments to look like they were effortless and meant to look that way, not look like a desperate attempt to cram a line of text in.

To change the margins, click on the Page Layout tab and look for the Margins button under the Page Setup grouping on the ribbon. When you click on the button, a menu with common margin sizes will appear. You can try one of the alternative preset options, like 'Narrow' or 'Moderate', or you can click on Custom Margins at the bottom of the menu to create your own custom margins. You do not need to worry about the Gutter or Gutter Position, as that is for print publishing.

Now, our next two formatting options can be applied as Page Formatting or Paragraph formatting.

Breaks

As much as possible, you don't want to start a section near the bottom of one page and then have it finish on the next page.

In the publishing industry, such text is called widows and orphans depending on whether the isolated detail appears on the first or the subsequent page. And just as it is actively avoided in publishing, we want to try to keep each of the specifics for a section with its section title and other specifics.

So, if your section is broken in half, you could look to see if changing the order of your sections around with another longer or shorter section that better matches the page space available would be your better option, or whether you may need to create an unusual amount of space at the bottom of the first page in order to push the section on to the next page.

You do not need to hit enter multiple times to do this. Actually, it is doing this that can mess up your formatting for other sections. The best way to force a section onto the next page is to use a Next Page Break. You will find the button for inserting a variety of different breaks on the Page Layout tab under the Page Setup grouping on the ribbon. Position the cursor in front of the first letter in your section title, and when you click on the button, which has a small icon of an arrow between two pages, you should choose the Next Page Break. You won't be able to insert any details into that blank-looking space on screen.

But if you turn on the Pilcrow, you'll see the words Section Break (Next Page) between double lines before and after those words at the end of the text before the break occurred.

Inserting breaks into documents can be a great source of frustration to people when they can't see the hidden formatting – because they are trying to do something, and Word seems to want to do something completely different. I recommend that if you are going to use breaks in your resume, then leave this until one of the last formatting you do before finishing your document, to save on unforseen hassles.

Columns

Our next Page and or Paragraph formatting option is Columns.

To be perfectly honest, the Functional Resume doesn't really have any word or short phrase bullet lists, unless you have included one or more of the optional resume sections, like tools of the trade, or social media savviness. But if you do have them, then using columns is a great way to reclaim wasted space.

You never want to create a bullet list that ends up as a massive list going down the page. Instead, you should try to balance the specifics by putting them into 2 or 3 columns.

To change your bullet point into columns, highlight each of the items in your bullet list, and the click on the Page Layout tab and look for the Columns button under the Page Setup grouping on the ribbon. Choose either 2 or 3 columns depending on what you think would work best.

Now, it is important to note here that when you use columns like this, you are automatically inserting Section Breaks into your document, and if you make changes to the text in your bullet list, especially if it is the first or last item in your bullet list, it can cause your formatting to do weird and unwanted things. Turn your Pilcrow tool on, and you'll see the hidden formatting.

Okay, now let's move on to the first of our Paragraph formatting options.

Line Spacing

The default setting for line spacing in Microsoft Word is the depth of 1.15, and we kept that default line spacing in our template too. But, if necessary, this is something, if you get really desperate, you could change to increase or decrease how much content you get onto a single page.

So, pretty much, setting the line spacing to exactly (1) one bunches the lines of text too close together that it interferes with readability, and adjusting it to double spacing makes the text too far apart. But, small changes might help, like changing from 1.15 to 1.20 etc.

To do this, you will find the Line Spacing button on the Home table under the Paragraph grouping on the ribbon. The icon has an up and down arrow on the left side of lines (which represent text). When you click on the button, you access a hidden dropdown menu, and you'll see that there is an orange button with a tick in front of the 1.15 option, which indicates that the 1.15 preset is currently being used. You could change the line spacing to 1.5, 2.0, 2.5, or 3.0 presets, where 2.0 is double and 3.0 is triple the line spacing, or you can click on the words Line Spacing Options to access the submenu options box.

Just over halfway down the options box, you will see a grouping called Spacing, and on the right hand side, under the word 'At' the number 1.15. You can enter a different and custom size by overtyping, as using the little up and down arrows will just cycle you through the presets which you could have changed back in the original dropdown menu when you click on the icon in the home tab ribbon.

Like I said, I don't often use this tool to achieve creating a 1 page resume, but I do occasionally use it when I need to 'fluff' or 'pad' the resume details out to make it a 2 page, when the information is a little short and I am unable to add additional details to existing bullets or include a section.

Space Before / Space After

Now the tool that will be most helpful to you towards adjusting the space is the Space Before and or the 'Space After' options. It is accessed from using the Line Spacing button, which we found on the Home tab under the Paragraph grouping in the ribbon.

Desktop publishers don't manually create gaps between paragraphs or headings by using pressing the enter key twice like most home users do; instead, they take a bit of time to set up the document's paragraph settings to how they want it look and work before they start adding text and graphics, and their use of the Space Before and Space After feature automatically creates the set amount of white space gaps for them.

The 2 resume electronic resume templates that we have included as part of this course both use Space After but not Space Before formatting, so if you activate the Pilcrow, you'll notice that the enter key has only been used once but there is still a larger amount of space between the sections.

If you really needed to, you could make that space slightly wider to stretch out your information, or reduce it to squeeze it closer together just by adjusting the point size – but, if you do this, then you need to apply the changes consistently, or the inconsistent amount of spacing will become noticeable.

The default Space Before and Space After setting when no Space Before or Space After is applied to text is 0 pt. And the default setting when the space is activated is 6 pt. If you use the up arrow to increase the spacing size, you'll notice that it goes up or down by 6 pt increments. That it, it goes 6, 12, 18 etc.

And, like with everything else in Microsoft Word, you don't have to use any of Microsoft's presets, you can assign your own. So, you could make it 4 pt or 8 pt to increase or decrease the gaps between sections and paragraphs.

Tabs & Indentations

Another little tool, that I almost forgot about, but which I use quite frequently is indents – increasing and decreasing options.

Margins are the white space that surrounds the body text area, like a lineless border. But, if we were to draw a line around the body text area, you would create a rectangle because you end up with 4 straight lines. Normally, if you want to change the margin, you do so for the full page, but we don't always want our text to be boxy like that. Sometimes, we want a small portion of the text to be narrower or wider than the margins. And one way to achieve that stepping out of the norm is to use indents.

Increasing Indent

Let's say you have included a Career Objective type section (but you are not including a typical career objective though) and your sentence is only 2 lines long, and you think it would look better visually if it was presented as 3 lines of text instead. Well, this is where you could adjust just that one paragraph to have different 'margins' to the rest of the document – which is an example of increasing indent.

But rather than messing with section breaks to create different page margins, simply highlight the text, and then adjust the margins for that selection of text only.

Now, like a lot of other tools that come with Microsoft Word, there are a couple of different ways to achieve the same thing, so I'm going to show you the simple and easiest way.

See these little markets on the ruler? This is the quickest way to make your adjustment.

So, with your text still highlighted, indent the left margin by 1.5 cm by sliding the little box rather than the arrow pointing up or down, as the box will drag both the up and down arrows together. You could do the arrows separately, instead and that's how you create first line and hanging indent text. Then, with your text still highlighted, slide the arrow pointing up on the right hand side of the ruler and slide it in by 1.5 cm. So there you go, you've increased the indent.

Now, of course that is the manual way of doing it, and maybe you want to be more precise. To access the options box, simply click on the tiny more options icon in the Paragraph grouping in the ribbon on the Home tab to open the same dialogue box you open by clicking on the Line Spacing icon and choosing Line Spacing Options. Either type in the measurement of how much you want to indent by, or use the little up or down arrows. You can make adjustments to just the left margin, just the right or both.

Decreasing Indent

Now, what you often find is that when you use the bullet or numbers list buttons, the items in your bullet or numbered list automatically is indented.

That is really useful at making the bullet list stand out in long text filled documents, but in our resume that indent space sometimes takes up valuable space, and sometimes causes the bullet point to become two lines of text because the last word didn't happen to fit by a character or two, and Microsoft Word automatically text wraps the word down to the next line.

You'll notice that the resume templates bullet points all sit at the left margin. That's because I decreased the indent.

To do this, you will find both the increase and decrease buttons in the Paragraph grouping in the ribbon of the Home tab. Click on the bullet list button, or highlight a group of existing bullet lists, and then click the decrease indent button to send it back to flush with the left margin.

The increase and decrease buttons control the left margin only. That's why I got you to use the ruler marking when increasing indent for the right margin.

Okay, so that is a brief explanation on the paragraph formatting tools that you could use to manipulate the text in your resume. The last thing we could do is to apply some text formatting options.

I'm only going to talk about the text formatting that you could use to adjust the text on the page to try and make it fit, this is not a lesson on how to use Microsoft Word in its entirety so I'm not going to go into the how's and whys of highlighting as emphasis to makes your text elements stand out but doesn't affect fitting text onto the page, like bolding, italicising, underlining and colouring text.

Font

The first one is the font chosen.

One font at size 12 can be vastly different in size compared to another font at size 12. Take for example the font Ministry Script compared to Engravers MT.

The font you choose needs to be a professional business communication font, like Times New Roman (which Graphic Designers all seem to hate), and which is a serif font, meaning it has all the little embellishing strokes that help to make the letters readable; or you could use a professional sans serif font, like Arial, which means it doesn't have any of the little embellishing strokes.

The general consensus of readability that I can gather seems to be: use a serif font when the document will be read on paper, and a sans serif when viewed on screen. But, maybe I'm just old school, because I am always more attracted to resumes that use Times New Roman or Garamond – which are both serif fonts, and I seem to always dislike resumes that use Calibri (though, I'm not sure whether that is because of the font, or because that font is the default font in Microsoft Word, and is found in nearly every resume I have had to fix up where the person has low computer skills and has been struggling with getting work for a long time that it has become a hallmark of a poor resume).

Changing the font you have used is likely to throw out how your text fits on the page, because in one font a line of text might end a space or two before the right margin but in a different font the same line of text is one and a half lines of text.

So, I recommend that you choose the font that you like best first and then make other formatting adjustments, rather than fit all your text in and apply all your formatting, and then go for a font change.

Font Size

But, while I don't recommend changing the font at the last minute, the last thing that can subtly give you the space you need, or fill up gaps is by changing the font size.

Start with just your name first. The template has sized your name to 18 pt. But you could increase that to size 24 pt if you want to, because a common best practice in resume writing is to not size your name any larger than double your body text size. As standard business communication uses Times New Roman at Size 12 pt, that is your starting point for what is easily readable – smaller and you start causing people with vision problems issues, larger and the text starts looking out of place.

Next, if you still need to gain or lose space, is adjusting the font size for your section headings. It would look silly to make them smaller than your body text, so your option here is more that you could fluff out your resume slightly by increasing the font size. We have kept the Section Titles sized at 12 pt, and you wouldn't want to increase the font size any more than size 14. Sometimes we make Section titles size 13 pt, which, when you look at the drop down menu isn't one of the presets, but we do this by typing 13 into the font size box in the Font grouping on the ribbon of the Home tab.

We don't recommend using a smaller font for body text because of the readability problems that it can cause. However, there is one exception to this, and that is the information contained in the documents header and footer area, if you use it. You can go as small as size 8 pt and people with good eyesight will be able to read small portions of text like this without any difficulty.

Just remember if you change the formatting of one section title then remember to do that for the rest of them.

So that is it for the formatting pro-techniques. We hope you have found the tips and techniques helpful, and we hope you have fun playing around with the formatting of your resume, as you put your personalisation to it.

YOUR ONE THING

At the beginning of this course, I asked you to think about what the one thing is about creating a resume that if you learned it would make this course all worth it for you.

Well, you've completed the course, hopefully having learned quite a lot about how to create a resume, so it's time to revisit that.

What did you write down when I originally asked you that question?

Please look back at your answer and take a moment to reflect upon what you've learned throughout our resume creating journey together.

Did we answer your particular one thing within this course?

As you know, we've worked really hard to ensure we share our best resume writing and hiring knowledge with you; but as you can also well appreciate, we can't pack everything we know in or the course would become too long and boring for anyone to get through, let alone finish it.

But, we want to make sure you got what you came for!

So:

If we have successfully resolved that most essential question for you, then we would love for you to tell us this – because knowing whether we successfully answered your most important question is our most important question. So if we were successful and answered your question, then please tell us this by leaving a message in the comments box below this video, so we know we got some things right.

If we haven't answered that one singlemost important question you held when you first started this course, then we want to answer it for you right now. That's right, our students are that important to us. We don't want any person to finish this course not having got the answer to that one important thing that would make the entire course worth it to them.

So, if we haven't already answered your one thing, please email us right now!

Note: You can use the Contact form on Char Mesan and the $\mathcal{S}$avvy $\mathcal{J}$obseeker $\mathcal{A}$cademy blog website.

We know your question must be a good one; and therefore, we will do our absolute best to provide you with the answer in the quickest time possible.

You never know; if we feel that other students would benefit from gaining the answer to your one thing too, we may even turn the answer to your one thing into create a video tutorial and add it to the course for everyone to benefit from!

So, thank you, everyone, for actively participating. *T*eam *S*avvy looks forward to reading your comments or emails!

CELEBRATE Your SUCCESS

While creating the video-based training, we received feedback from a few beta testing students who suggested that we create an online page inside the course where students can share their jobsearch success with *Team Savvy* and other students.

We thought that was FANTASTIC idea, so we did just that. And we invited students to leave a Comment in the forums, so those jobseekers that visited the page after them, especially those that are still struggling and haven't achieved success yet could find inspiration and positivity from reading about your success.

The page enables *Team Savvy* to congratulate those who share their 'wins', and we encourage students to share big and small successes, like finishing creating your new resume, nailing a job interview, nailing a job offer – with the only rule being no negative comments (because there is already more than enough negativity happening in many jobseekers personal lives so we actively wish to create a positive place they can escape to and take comfort from).

And, just because you decided to purchase the print publication instead of enrolling in the online course doesn't mean you should miss out on being able to share your positive experiences with others. So, if you feel so inclined, please visit my Facebook Page (Char Mesan) and use the Review (you'll need to give us a rating too though, which we hope you will make it 5 stars!) and then you can Comment.

So, don't be shy. Why not let everyone know!

Oh, and please: if you do have negative comments, please email them to us privately, so we can resolve whatever the issue is (or at least try to) first.

More from Char Mesan and
The Savvy Jobseeker Academy

If you would like some more inspiration to help you while you look for work, then please visit the Savvy Jobseeker Academy eCourses page. Click on my Trainer Profile to see what other free and paid courses that I teach for **Team Savvy** – including The Job Seek Motivator (which is also available as a Kindle book on Amazon.com).

COURSES
Available Now

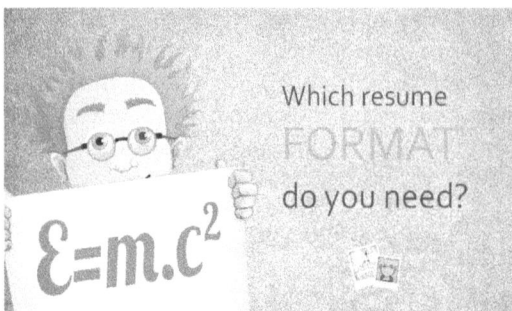

Which resume FORMAT do you need?

Coming Soon

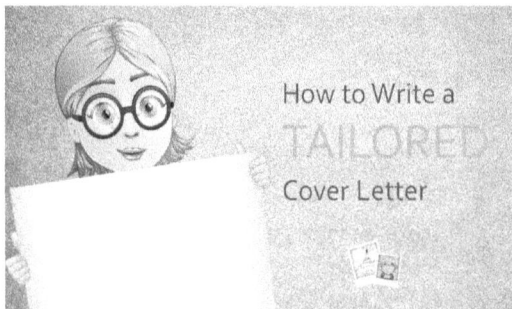

How to Write a TAILORED Cover Letter

BOOKS
Available Now

- Amazon
- Apple
- Barnes & Noble
- Google Play
- And other online bookstores

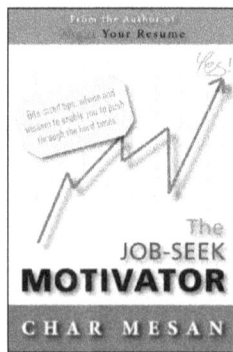

Leave a REVIEW

If you found the information in How to Create a Functional Resume helpful, please support the creators by leaving a review with the retailer you purchased the book from or at Char Mesan's Facebook Page.

Thank you

FUNCTIONAL RESUME MASTER WORKSHEET

Do not complete until instructed to do so.

1.1	Email:	
	Mobile:	

'Career Objective' (which I will entitle as _____)

5.4	

CORE SKILLS (which I will entitle as _____)

9.9	•
	•
	•
	•
	•
	•
	•
	•

FUNCTIONAL RESUME MASTER WORKSHEET

PERSONAL PROFILE (which I will entitle as _____)

10.9	
	•
	•
	•
	•
	•
	•
	•
	•

OTHER RELEVANT SECTION 01 – if required
(which I will entitle as _____)

13.6	
	•
	•
	•
	•
	•
	•
	•
	•

FUNCTIONAL RESUME MASTER WORKSHEET

OTHER RELEVANT SECTION 02 – if required
(which I will entitle as _____)

13.6	•
	•
	•
	•
	•
	•
	•
	•

OTHER RELEVANT SECTION 03 – if required
(which I will entitle as _____)

	•
	•
	•
	•
	•
	•
	•
	•

FUNCTIONAL RESUME MASTER WORKSHEET

QUALIFICATIONS & REQUIREMENTS (1) – (Licensing, Tickets & Checks)
(which I will entitle as _____)

11.3	Graduate or Enrollee	Course, Qualification or Licensing Title

QUALIFICATIONS & REQUIREMENTS (2) – (Training & Education)
(which I will entitle as _____)

11.3	Graduate or Enrollee	Course, Qualification or Licensing Title

FUNCTIONAL RESUME MASTER WORKSHEET

EMPLOYMENT & DEVELOPMENT
(which I will entitle as _____)

12.1	Position Title	Company Name	Started (Month & Year	Finished (Month & Year)

REFEREES - (Optional)

11.3	Name	Company

FUNCTIONAL RESUME MASTER WORKSHEET

AWARDS & ACHIEVEMENTS

11.3 Name	Issued by

Congratulations!

You have now successfully created the CONTENT for your Functional Format Resume.

Before you move on to creating your electronic document please watch any remaining course lessons and tutorials.

www.ingramcontent.com/pod-product-compliance
Lightning Source LLC
Chambersburg PA
CBHW080525220326
41599CB00032B/6201